Nick Vandome

Windows 10

5th edition

In easy steps is an imprint of In Easy Steps Limited
16 Hamilton Terrace · Holly Walk · Leamington Spa
Warwickshire · United Kingdom · CV32 4LY
www.ineasysteps.com

Fifth Edition

Notice of Liability
Every effort has been made to ensure that this book contains accurate
and current information. However, In Easy Steps Limited and the
author shall not be liable for any loss or damage suffered by readers
as a result of any information contained herein.

Trademarks
Microsoft® and Windows® are registered trademarks of Microsoft
Corporation. All other trademarks are acknowledged as belonging to
their respective companies.

In Easy Steps Limited supports The Forest Stewardship Council (FSC),
the leading international forest certification organization. All our titles
that are printed on Greenpeace approved FSC certified paper carry the
FSC logo.

MIX
Paper from
responsible sources
FSC® C020837
FSC
www.fsc.org

Printed and bound in the United Kingdom

ISBN 978-1-84078-892-1

Contents

1 Introducing Windows 10   7

What is Windows?	8
About Windows 10	9
About the November 2019 Update	10
Windows 10 Interface	12
Obtaining Windows 10	14
Keyboard Shortcuts	15
Windows 10 for Touch	16
Control Panel and Settings	17
Using a Microsoft Account	18
Sign-in Options	20

2 Getting Started   23

The Start Button	24
The Start Menu	26
Versions of the Start Menu	28
Customizing the Start Menu	30
Working with Groups	32
Resizing Tiles	34
Creating Folders	35
The Desktop and Taskbar	36
Shutting Down	37
Task View and Timeline	38
Adding a Phone	41
Notifications	42
Focus Assist	44
Settings	46
Searching	62
Setting Up Cortana	64
Using Cortana	65
Adding and Switching Users	68

3 Working with Apps   71

Starting with Apps	72
Windows 10 Apps	74
Using Windows 10 Apps	76
Classic Apps on the Desktop	78
Closing Apps	79
Viewing All Apps	80
Searching for Apps	81
Pin to Start Menu	82
Pin to Taskbar	83
Using the Microsoft Store	84
Buying Apps	87
Viewing Your Apps	88
Using Live Tiles	89
Install and Uninstall	90
Task Manager	92

Standard Controls 93

Menus	94
Dialog Boxes	95
Structure of a Window	96
Moving a Window	97
Restoring a Window	98
Resizing a Window	99
Arranging Windows	100
Snap Assist	102
Using Multiple Windows	104
Switching Windows	106
Arranging Icons	107
Closing a Window	108

Customizing Windows 109

Personalization	110
Using Themes	112
Changing Color Themes	114
Lock Screen Settings	116
Changing Sound	118
Desktop Icons	119
Screen Resolution	120
Managing Storage	121
Ease of Access	122
Date and Time Functions	124

File Explorer 125

Opening File Explorer	126
The Taskbar	127
Libraries	128
Scenic Ribbon	129
This PC Folder	131
Quick Access	132
Exploring Drives	134
Address Bar	136
Navigation Panes	138
Changing Views	140
Sorting	141
Filtering	142
Grouping	143
Folder Options	144

7   Managing Files and Folders   145

Select Files and Folders   146
Copy or Move Files or Folders   148
File Conflicts   152
Open Files   153
Delete Files and Folders   154
The Recycle Bin   155
Create a Folder   158
Rename a File or Folder   159
Backtrack File Operations   160
File Properties   161
Search for Files and Folders   162
Compressed Folders   163

8   Digital Lifestyle   165

Using OneDrive   166
OneDrive Settings   169
Viewing Photos   170
Editing Photos   172
Groove Music   174
Playing Music   175
Viewing Movies and TV   176
Using Paint 3D   178
Gaming with Windows 10   179

9   Microsoft Edge Browser   181

About the Edge Browser   182
Smart Address Bar   183
Setting a Homepage   184
Using Tabs   185
Bookmarking Web Pages   188
Adding Notes to Web Pages   189
Organizing with the Hub   191
Reading List   192
Reading View   193
More Options   194

10   Keeping in Touch   195

Setting Up Mail   196
Working with Mail   198
Chatting with Skype   200
Finding People   202
Using the Calendar   204

11 Networking and Sharing 207

Network Components	208
Connecting to a Network	209
Viewing Network Status	210
Nearby Sharing	212
Sharing Settings	214
View Network Components	215
Network Troubleshooting	216

12 System and Security 217

Privacy	218
Troubleshooting	219
System Properties	220
Clean Up Your Disk	222
Windows Update	224
Backing Up	227
System Restore	228
Windows Security	230

Index 233

1 Introducing Windows 10

This chapter explains what Windows is, and shows how to get started with the operating system, including the enhancements in the Windows 10 November 2019 Update and its interface, keyboard shortcuts, and creating and using a Microsoft Account.

8   What is Windows?

9   About Windows 10

10   About the November 2019 Update

12   Windows 10 Interface

14   Obtaining Windows 10

15   Keyboard Shortcuts

16   Windows 10 for Touch

17   Control Panel and Settings

18   Using a Microsoft Account

20   Sign-in Options

What is Windows?

Windows is an operating system made by Microsoft, for PCs (personal computers), laptops and tablets. The operating system is the software that organizes and controls all of the components (hardware and software) in your computer.

The first operating system from Microsoft was known as MS-DOS (Microsoft Disk Operating System). This was a non-graphical, line-oriented, command-driven operating system, able to run only one application at a time. The original Windows system was an interface manager that ran on top of the MS-DOS system, providing a graphical user interface (GUI) and using clever processor and memory management to allow it to run more than one application or function at a time.

The basic element of Windows was its "windowing" capability. A window (with a lower-case w) is a rectangular area used to display information or to run a program or app. Several windows can be opened at the same time so that you can work with multiple applications. This provided a dramatic increase in productivity, in comparison with the original MS-DOS.

Between 1985-2000 Microsoft released six versions of this interface management Windows, with numerous intermediate versions.

- 1985 – Windows 1.0. ● 1987 – Windows 2.0, 2.1 & 2.11.
- 1990 – Windows 3.0, 3.1, 3.11 (Windows for Workgroups).
- 1995 – Windows 95.
- 1998 – Windows 98, 98 SE.
- 2000 – Windows Me (Millennium Edition).

In 2001 Windows XP was introduced, which was a full operating system in its own right. This was followed by Windows Vista and then Windows 7, 8, 8.1 and 10 (there was no Windows 9). Although Windows 10 has been in operation since 2015, there has been no numerical update to the operating system. Instead of releasing Windows 11, 12, etc., each new version has been given a Windows 10 title – e.g. the Windows 10 Anniversary Update, the Windows 10 Creators Update. The latest version – the Windows 10 November 2019 Update – continues the naming convention that was started with the Windows 10 April 2018 version that used a date to identify the update, thus making it easier to identify which version of the software you are using – the Windows 10 November 2019 Update is more time-specific than the Windows 10 Creators Update.

The New icon pictured above indicates a new or enhanced feature introduced with the Windows 10 November 2019 Update. (Some of these updates were included with the May 2019 Update, but for the sake of consistency are included under the November 2019 Update, to cover all of the updates since the last edition of the book.)

About Windows 10

The latest version of Windows was released in November 2019:

- 2019 – Windows 10 November 2019 Update, which can be used to upgrade any existing version of Windows 10.

All major computer operating systems (OS) undergo regular upgrades and new versions. Sometimes these are a significant visual overhaul, while others concentrate more on the behind-the-scenes aspect of the OS. In terms of Microsoft Windows, Windows 8 was one of the most radical updates to the User Interface (UI), and introduced a number of new features for both desktop and mobile versions of Windows. However, it was not met with universal approval, as it was perceived that it was two separate operating systems (desktop and mobile) bolted together, and not satisfying either environment completely.

With Windows 10, a lot of the problems with Windows 8 were addressed: the familiar Start menu was reinstated to return to a UI similar to earlier versions of Windows; there was a greater consolidation between desktop and mobile devices running Windows 10; and the operation of apps was standardized so that it is similar for the new Windows apps as well as the more traditional ones. In a sense, this was a case of going back one step in order to go forwards two steps, and Windows 10 has succeeded in creating a familiar environment, coupled with a range of innovative and useful features.

Windows 10 November 2019 Update

The intention for Windows 10 has always been to produce incremental updates, rather than waiting a period of time for the next major update. This is the reason why it is unlikely that there will be a Windows 11; instead, there will be regular online updates to Windows 10. The Windows 10 November 2019 Update contains a number of improvements and refinements but, in keeping with the Windows 10 ethos, it is an incremental update rather than a major new operating system, although it contains a comprehensive range of new features. The November 2019 Update is delivered online through the Windows Update function in the Settings app, or the Windows 10 Update Assistant app. A registered version of Windows 10 has to be installed in order for the November 2019 Update to be downloaded (or a license can be bought when downloading the Windows 10 November 2019 Update).

The functionality of the November 2019 Update is generally the same as for the original Windows 10, and it will, in general, be referred to as Windows 10 throughout the book.

Windows 10 has had a number of updates since it was released in July 2015. In general, there are two updates a year, and for the purposes of this book, the November 2019 Update represents the completion of the fifth annual update.

About the November 2019 Update

The Windows 10 November 2019 Update is an extension of the May 2019 Update, which was the major update for 2019 in terms of the user interface and the operating system's functionality. Some of the additions and enhancements that have been incorporated into the November 2019 Update include:

These features are new or updated in the Windows 10 November 2019 Update.

- **Light Theme**. This is a new theme that provides a lighter color scheme for the Windows 10 background and associated items, including the Start menu and the Taskbar. It is applied with the **Personalization > Colors** section of the **Settings** app.

- **Start menu**. The Start menu has been redesigned so that the right-hand section, containing the colored tiles that are shortcuts to their related apps, is in one column, as opposed to the previous two columns. However, this only applies for new PCs and laptops that are bought with the Windows 10 November 2019 Update, or new accounts that are created on an existing device.

See pages 28-29 for more details about the different version of the Start menu.

10

- **Windows Update**. In the Settings app there is now a greater range of options for how updates to Windows 10 are handled, giving you more control over the update process.

The November 2019 Update includes all of the elements that were introduced in the May 2019 Update.

- **Uninstalling built-in apps**. It is now possible to uninstall a greater number of the built-in Windows apps, to make the Start menu less cluttered with apps that you do not need.

- **Cortana and Search box separated**. In earlier versions of Windows 10, the Search box and the button for the digital voice assistant, Cortana, were grouped together. In the Windows 10 November 2019 Update they are now separated, but still next to each other on the Taskbar, with the Cortana button to the right of the Search box.

- **Accounts without passwords**. Instead of having to enter a password every time you need to unlock your PC or laptop, it is now possible to set up an account so that it can be unlocked with a variety of options.

- **Speed improvements**. The Windows 10 November 2019 Update introduces a range of behind-the-scenes speed improvements for launching apps and overall performance.

Windows 10 Interface

Windows 8 was one of the most significant changes to the Windows operating system since Windows 95 helped redefine the way that we look at personal computers. It aimed to bring the desktop and mobile computing environments together, principally with the brightly colored Start screen and Charms bar. However, this proved to be awkward for a lot of users, with Windows 8 not fully meeting the needs of the device being used.

The original Windows 10 interface was redesigned so that it looks as similar as possible, regardless of whether it is being used on a desktop computer with a mouse and keyboard, or on a mobile or touchscreen device (and most of the underlying functionality is still the same). The first major upgrade of Windows 10 – the Anniversary Update – saw one significant change, in that the operating system recognized the type of device being used and amended the interface accordingly. The Windows 10 November 2019 Update keeps the same interface as the previous annual update of Windows 10, but with enhancements to the overall color theme of the user interface and a streamlined version of the Start menu for some users (see pages 28-29 for details).

As with the original Windows 10, the November 2019 Update opens at the Desktop, where shortcuts to items can be placed, and the Taskbar is at the bottom of the screen. This is the default view when opening Windows 10.

The main recommended specifications for PCs and laptops running the Windows 10 November 2019 Update are: 1GHz processor; 1GB RAM (32-bit Windows) or 2GB RAM (64-bit Windows); and 16GB (32-bit Windows) or 20GB (64-bit Windows) of free disk space for installation.

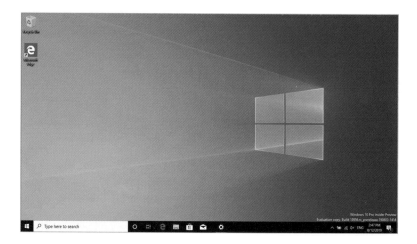

Start menu

The Start menu was reinstated in the original version of Windows 10, although it now includes a range of colored tiles that can be pinned to the Start menu and used to access the most commonly used or favorite apps. The left-hand side of the Start menu contains links to some of your most frequently used functions, such as the Power button, the Settings app, the File Explorer, the Most used apps, and the alphabetic list of all of the apps on the PC.

The Settings app can be used to customize the Start menu (**Settings > Personalization > Start**). See page 51 for more details.

The Windows 10 November 2019 Update has an updated default Start menu, if it is on a new PC or laptop, or a new user account on an existing one. (See pages 28-29 for more details.)

Windows 10 for touchscreen

The Windows 10 version that is optimized for touchscreen use is designed for use with a tablet (such as the Microsoft Surface Pro), where all of the screen navigation can be done by

tapping, swiping and pinching on the screen. These features can also be used on touchscreen desktops and laptops that have this functionality (see page 16 for details). Some tablets also have a detachable keyboard that can be used with standard controls.

13

Obtaining Windows 10

Windows 10 is an online service, rather than just a stand-alone operating system. This means that by default, Windows 10 is obtained and downloaded online, with subsequent updates and upgrades also provided online on a regular basis.

Windows 10 can be bought and downloaded from the Microsoft website or through software retailers as a disc. A registered version of Windows 10 has to be installed before the free November 2019 Update can be downloaded, unless a PC is running Windows 7 or 8, in which case it can be upgraded to the November 2019 Update if a license is bought. The options for obtaining the Windows 10 November 2019 Update are:

For more information about the Settings app, see pages 46-61.

- **Use Windows Update** – replace an older version of Windows 10, retaining the installed applications and settings. This can be done through the **Settings** app (select **Update & Security** > **Windows Update** and click on the **Check for updates** button).

- **Use the Windows 10 Update Assistant app** – this can be accessed from the Start menu (see pages 26-27 for details about using the Start menu).

- **Microsoft website** – visit the software download page on the Microsoft website (**microsoft.com/en-us/software-download/windows10**) to use the **Update Assistant** to download the Windows 10 November 2019 Update.

- **Preinstall** – buy a new PC or laptop with the Windows 10 November 2019 Update already installed.

Some of the steps that the installation will go through are:

- **Personalize**. These are settings that will be applied to your version of Windows 10. These settings can also be selected within the Settings app once Windows 10 has been installed.

- **Settings**. You can choose to have express settings applied, or customize them.

- **Microsoft Account**. You can set up a Microsoft Account during installation, or once you have started Windows 10.

- **Privacy**. Certain privacy settings can be applied during the setup process for Windows 10.

14

Keyboard Shortcuts

As you become more confident using Windows 10 you may want to access certain items more quickly. There are a range of keyboard shortcuts that can be used to access some of the items you use most frequently.

The majority of the shortcuts are accessed together with the WinKey (Windows key) on the keyboard. To use the keyboard shortcuts press:

- **WinKey** to access the Start menu at any time.

- **WinKey** + **L** to lock the computer and display the Lock screen.

- **WinKey** + **I** to access the Settings app.

- **WinKey** + **K** to connect new devices.

- **WinKey** + **Q** to access the Search window.

- **WinKey** + **D** to access the Desktop.

- **WinKey** + **M** to access the Desktop with the active window minimized.

- **WinKey** + **E** to access File Explorer, displaying the Quick access section.

- **WinKey** + **T** to display the thumbnails on the Desktop Taskbar.

- **WinKey** + **U** to access the Ease of Access options in the Settings app.

- **WinKey** + **X** to access the Power User menu, which gives you quick access to items including the Desktop and File Explorer.

- **Alt** + **F4** to close a Windows 10 app.

- **Ctrl** + **Shift** + **Esc** to access the Task Manager.

Windows 10 for Touch

One of the aims of Windows 10 is to make the operating system more familiar again to users with a keyboard and mouse. This has been done by reverting back to a more traditional look and feel than that of Windows 8 and 8.1. For touchscreen devices such as tablets and laptops with precision touchpads, the same overall operation of Windows 10 has been maintained so that users can feel comfortable with the operating system regardless of the device on which they are using it.

Continuum

Continuum refers to the function of Windows 10 where you can start something on one Windows 10 device and then continue working on it on another. For instance, you could start a letter in Word on a desktop computer, save it, and then pick up where you left off on the Microsoft tablet, Surface. Continuum works between desktop computers, laptops and tablets.

Using touch

Touchscreen devices and those with precision touchpads can be used with Windows 10 to navigate through a number of gestures, swipes and taps on the screen or touchpad. The range of these gestures has been consolidated from Windows 8 and 8.1, since these included a number of options for accessing the Charms that are no longer available with Windows 10. Some of the gestures that can be used with touchscreen or touchpad devices using Windows 10 are:

Hot tip

Aside from the gestures used on a touchscreen device, much of the operation of Windows 10 has been consolidated between computers with a mouse and keyboard, and mobile devices.

- Swipe inwards from the right-hand edge to access the Notification area (Action Center).

- Swipe inwards from the left-hand edge to access the Task View for currently open apps, and the Timeline.

- In an open Windows 10 app, swipe downwards from the top of the screen to access the app's toolbar.

- In an open Windows 10 app, use a long swipe downwards from the top of the screen to close the app.

- Swipe upwards from the bottom of the screen to access the Taskbar (when an app is at full screen).

- Tap with three fingers on a touchpad to bring up the personal digital assistant, Cortana.

Control Panel and Settings

In previous versions of Windows, the Control Panel played an important role in applying settings for a number of different functions. Because of this, it could be accessed in several different ways. However, in the Windows 10 November 2019 Update, more of the Control Panel functionality has been moved to the Settings app, and there are fewer methods for accessing the Control Panel. Despite this, it can still be used to access a variety of settings:

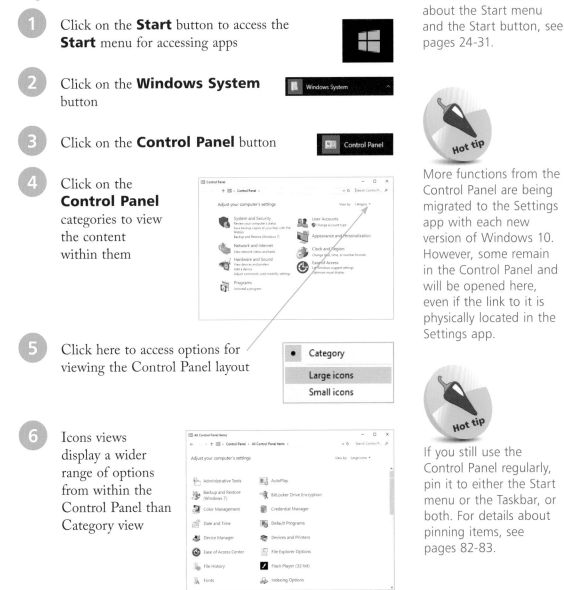

1 Click on the **Start** button to access the **Start** menu for accessing apps

2 Click on the **Windows System** button

3 Click on the **Control Panel** button

4 Click on the **Control Panel** categories to view the content within them

5 Click here to access options for viewing the Control Panel layout

6 Icons views display a wider range of options from within the Control Panel than Category view

Don't forget

For more information about the Start menu and the Start button, see pages 24-31.

Hot tip

More functions from the Control Panel are being migrated to the Settings app with each new version of Windows 10. However, some remain in the Control Panel and will be opened here, even if the link to it is physically located in the Settings app.

Hot tip

If you still use the Control Panel regularly, pin it to either the Start menu or the Taskbar, or both. For details about pinning items, see pages 82-83.

Using a Microsoft Account

We live in a world of ever-increasing computer connectivity, where users expect to be able to access their content wherever they are and share it with their friends and family in a variety of ways, whether it is by email, messaging or photo sharing. This is known as Cloud computing, with content being stored on online servers, from where it can be accessed by authorized users.

In Windows 10, this type of connectivity is achieved with a Microsoft Account. This is a registration system (which can be set up with most email addresses and a password) that provides access to a number of services via the Windows 10 apps. These include:

Without a Microsoft Account you will not be able to access the full functionality of the apps listed here.

- **Mail**. This is the Windows 10 email app that can be used to access and manage your different email accounts.

- **Skype**. This is the text messaging and video chatting app.

- **People**. This is the address book app.

- **Calendar**. This is the calendar and organizer app.

- **Microsoft Store**. This is the online store for previewing and downloading additional apps.

- **OneDrive**. This is the online backup and sharing service.

Creating a Microsoft Account

It is free to create a Microsoft Account. This can be done with an email address and, together with a password, provides a unique identifier for logging in to your Microsoft Account and the related apps. There are several ways in which you can create and set up a Microsoft Account:

- During the initial setup process when you install Windows 10. You will be asked if you want to create a Microsoft Account at this point. If you do not, you can always do so at a later time.

- When you first open an app that requires access to a Microsoft Account. When you do this you will be prompted to create a new account.

- From the **Accounts** section of the **Settings** app (see page 53).

...cont'd

Whichever way you use to create a Microsoft Account, the process is similar:

1 When you are first prompted to sign in with a Microsoft Account you can enter your account details, if you have one, or

> **Make it yours**
>
> Your Microsoft account opens a world of benefits. Learn more
>
> Email, phone, or Skype name
>
> Password
>
> Forgot my password
>
> **No account?** Create one!
>
> Microsoft privacy statement
>
> Sign in

2 Click on the **No account? Create one!** link

> No account? Create one!

Hot tip

Microsoft Account details can also be used as your sign-in for Windows 10 (see pages 20-21).

19

3 Enter your name, an email address and a password for your Microsoft Account

> **Let's create your account**
>
> Windows, Office, Outlook.com, OneDrive, Skype, Xbox. They're all better and more personal when you sign in with your Microsoft account.* Learn more
>
> nickvandome@gmail.com   ×
>
> Get a new email address
>
> Password
>
> United Kingdom   ∨
>
> *If you already use a Microsoft service, go Back to sign in with that account.
>
> Next   Back

4 Click on the **Next** button to move through the registration process

> Next

5 Enter your password again to confirm your account

6 Click on the **Finish** button in the final window to complete setting up your Microsoft Account

> **Sign in to this device using your Microsoft account**
>
> From here on out, you'll unlock this device using either the password for your Microsoft account or, if you've set one up, your PIN. That way, you can get help from Cortana, you can find your device if you lose it, and your settings will automatically sync.
>
> To make sure it's really you, we'll need your current Windows password one last time. Next time you sign into Windows you'll use your Microsoft account password.
>
> If you don't have a Windows password, just leave the box blank and select Next.
>
> Current Windows password
>
> [   ]
>
> Next

Sign-in Options

Each time you start up your computer you will need to sign in. This is a security feature so that no-one can gain unauthorized access to your account on your PC. The sign-in process starts with the Lock screen and then you have to enter your sign-in password.

For details about personalizing the Lock screen, see page 51.

 When you start your PC the Lock screen will be showing. This is linked to the sign-in screen

11:27
Friday, April 28

You can lock your PC at any time by pressing **WinKey** + **L**.

Click on the **Lock screen**, or press any key to move to the sign-in screen. Enter your password and press **Enter**, or click on this arrow

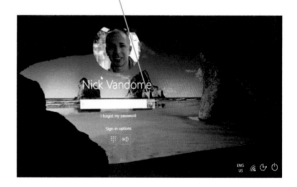

Nick Vandome

I forgot my password

Sign-in options

You will get an error message if you enter the wrong password or if you simply mis-key and cause an incorrect character to be added.

If you forget your password for your Microsoft Account, click on the **I forgot my password** link on the sign-in screen to reset it.

On the sign-in screen, click on this button to select Ease of Access options

On the sign-in screen, click on this button to select Power off options including Shut down and Restart

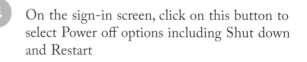

5 If there are other users with an account on the same PC, their names will be displayed here

Don't forget

You can sign in with a Local account or a Microsoft Account. If you sign in with the latter, you will have access to the related services, such as Mail and People. Also, you will be able to sync your settings and use them on another computer when you log in with your account.

6 Click on another user to access their own sign-in screen

Sign-in settings

Settings for how you sign in can be accessed from the Accounts section in the Settings app:

1 Access the **Settings** app and click on the **Accounts** button

Accounts
Your accounts, email, sync, work, family

2 Under **Sign-in options**, select options for how you sign in from the Lock screen

Sign-in options

Don't forget

For details about using the Settings app, see pages 46-61.

Sign-in options

Manage how you sign in to your device

Select a sign-in option to add, change, or remove it.

Windows Hello Face
This option is currently unavailable—click to learn more

Windows Hello Fingerprint
This option is currently unavailable—click to learn more

Windows Hello PIN
Sign in with a PIN (Recommended)

Security Key
Sign in with a physical security key

Password
Sign in with your account's password

Picture Password
Swipe and tap your favorite photo to unlock your device

Hot tip

Windows Hello Face and Windows Hello Fingerprint are functions that use biometric authentication for signing in to Windows 10. This is either done by scanning your face or with a fingerprint reader. However, specialist hardware is required and this is not available on many devices at present.

...cont'd

Using a PIN to sign in

Using a PIN to sign in to your Windows 10 computer can be an more convenient option than remembering a long password each time (although a password still has to be used when the account is created). To use a PIN to sign in:

1 Access the **Sign-in options** section of the Settings app, as shown on page 21, and click on the **Windows Hello PIN** option

::: Windows Hello PIN
Sign in with a PIN (Recommended)

2 Click on the **Add** button to create the new PIN

::: Windows Hello PIN
Sign in with a PIN (Recommended)
You can use this PIN to sign in to Windows, apps, and services.
Learn more
Add

3 Click on the **Next** button

Next

4 Enter the account password, to show that you are authorized to create a PIN for signing in to the account. Click on the **Sign in** button

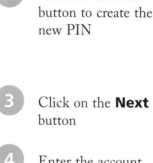

Microsoft
nickvandome@gmail.com
Enter password
Because you're accessing sensitive info, you need to verify your password.
Password
Forgot my password
Sign in

5 Enter the new PIN and enter it again to confirm it. Click on the **OK** button to finish setting up the PIN

Windows Security   ×
Set up a PIN
Create a PIN to use in place of passwords. Having a PIN makes it easier to sign in to your device, apps, and services.
New PIN
Confirm PIN
☐ Include letters and symbols
OK   Cancel

Don't forget

If you want to create a picture password for signing in you must have a touchscreen device. Select a picture and draw a pattern to use as your sign-in.

22

2 Getting Started

This chapter looks at some of the main features of Windows 10, focusing on the Start menu and its two different versions; using the Desktop and the Taskbar; and Task View, with the Timeline feature for viewing items that you have previously opened or edited (up to 30 days earlier). It also covers the personal digital assistant, Cortana, for voice searching over your computer for a range of items, and switching between users on your PC.

24 The Start Button

26 The Start Menu

28 Versions of the Start Menu

30 Customizing the Start Menu

32 Working with Groups

34 Resizing Tiles

35 Creating Folders

36 The Desktop and Taskbar

37 Shutting Down

38 Task View and Timeline

41 Adding a Phone

42 Notifications

44 Focus Assist

46 Settings

62 Searching

64 Setting Up Cortana

65 Using Cortana

68 Adding and Switching Users

The Start Button

The Start button has been a significant part of Windows computing for numerous versions of the operating system. There was a change in the traditional use of the Start button with the introduction of Windows 8, but this was met with widespread disapproval and the Start button has since been reinstated. In the Windows 10 November 2019 Update, the Start button works in a similar way to most early versions of Windows, with some enhancements.

Using the Start button

The Start button provides access to the apps on your Windows 10 PC and also to the enhanced Start menu:

 Click on the **Start** button in the bottom left-hand corner of the screen

 The **Start** menu is displayed

3 The left-hand side of the Start menu contains links to the most used apps, a list of quick links to items such as the Power button, and an alphabetic list of all of the apps on the computer

 The right-hand side of the Start menu is where apps can be pinned so that they are always available. These are displayed as a collection of large, colored tiles

 Other items can also be accessed from the Start button by right-clicking on it

...cont'd

Power User menu

In addition to accessing the Start menu, the Start button also provides access to the Power User menu, which can be accessed as follows:

1 Right-click on the **Start** button to view the Power User menu

Apps and Features
Mobility Center
Power Options
Event Viewer
System
Device Manager
Network Connections
Disk Management
Computer Management
Windows PowerShell
Windows PowerShell (Admin)
Task Manager
Settings
File Explorer
Search
Run
Shut down or sign out.   >
Desktop

2 Click on the relevant buttons to view items including the **Desktop** and other popular locations such as the **File Explorer**

The Start button Power User menu in Step 1 has a number of options for accessing system functions, such as Device Manager and Disk Management.

25

Task Manager
Settings
File Explorer
Search
Run
Shut down or sign out   >
Desktop

3 **Shut down or sign out** options are also available from the **Start** button (see page 37)

The Start Menu

The Start menu in Windows 10 is where you can access areas within your computer, perform certain functions, and also access apps from a variety of locations. Some of the default items on the Start menu can be customized to a certain extent (see pages 30-31) and there is considerable functionality here:

 Your most frequently used apps are displayed here. Click on one to open it (these items will change as you use different apps)

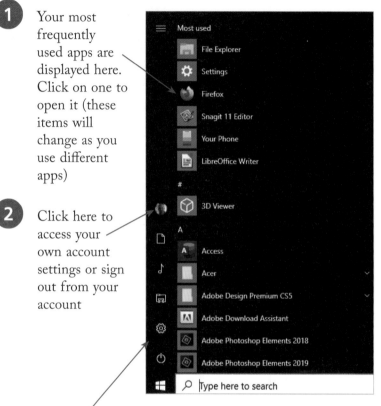

Hot tip

Click on this button to view a textual description for the items in the left-hand sidebar of the Start menu.

26

② Click here to access your own account settings or sign out from your account

③ Click here to access items including the **File Explorer**, your **Documents** library within File Explorer and the Windows 10 **Settings**

④ Click on the **Power** button for options to **Sleep** your computer, **Shut down** or **Restart**

Use the scroll bar at the right-hand side to move through the list of apps

The scroll bar only appears when you hover over that side of the panel with your mouse.

Click on a letter at the top of a section of apps to view an alphabetic grid. Click on a letter to move to that section.

 If there is a down-pointing arrow next to an app, this means that there are additional items that can be accessed. Click on the arrow to view these

Windows Accessories

Windows Accessories

3D Builder

Character Map

Math Input Panel

Notepad

Paint

27

Versions of the Start Menu

The Start menu in the Windows 10 November 2019 Update has been redesigned from previous versions: the right-hand section of the Start menu (containing the colored tiles) has been condensed into one column, as opposed to the two that were previously used. This makes the Start menu more streamlined.

The one-column Start menu is a new feature in the Windows 10 November 2019 Update.

- The Start menu is still located in the same location, except it only takes up one column. This makes it more compact and also reveals a greater amount of the Desktop area.

In terms of functionality, the two versions of the Start menu are very similar: even though the newer version only contains one column of tiles, its operation is the same as the two-column version.

- The new version of the Start menu can be organized in the same way as the previous one, with group headings and folders containing more than one app.

Previous version of the Start menu

Despite the new design for the Start menu in the November 2019 Update, Microsoft has recognized the fact that some users are more comfortable with a design with which they have become accustomed, containing two columns and taking up a greater area of the Desktop. Because of this, the new design is only available on new PCs or laptops with the November 2019 Update already installed, or if you create a new account on your existing PC or laptop (see below).

For details about adding more apps to the right-hand section of the Start menu, and also adding them to the Taskbar, see pages 82-83.

29

Adding a new account with the new Start menu

If a new account is added to an existing Windows 10 PC or laptop with the November 2019 Update, it will be created with the new version of the Start menu. To do this:

1 Open the **Settings** app and click on the **Accounts** button

Accounts
Your accounts, email, sync, work, family

2 Click on the **Family & other users** button

Family & other users

For more details about adding new users to your PC or laptop, and switching between them, see pages 68-70.

3 Select either **Add a family member** or **Add someone else to this PC** and complete the wizard to set up the new account

Add a family member

Add someone else to this PC

Customizing the Start Menu

Windows 10 is very adaptable and can be customized in several ways, so that it works best for you. This includes the Start menu, which can be set to behave in certain ways and have specific items added to it. To do this:

1 Open the **Settings** app and click on the **Personalization** button

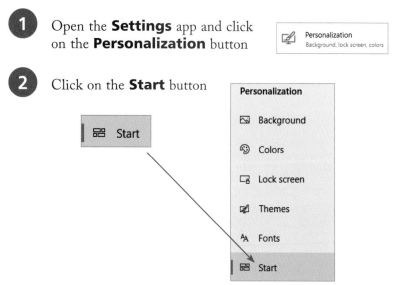

2 Click on the **Start** button

3 Under **Start**, select whether to show suggestions for apps on the Start menu, show recently added apps and most used apps on the Start menu, or show the Start menu in full screen

Beware

Full screen mode is designed more for tablets, and if you use it, the Start menu will occupy the whole screen.

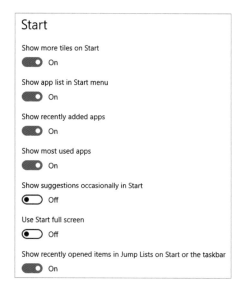

4 Click on the **Choose which folders appear on Start** button to select the items that appear on the Start menu

5 Drag the buttons **On** for the items you want to appear on the Start menu; i.e. the File Explorer, the Settings app, the Documents library, and the Music app

⚙ Choose which folders appear on Start

File Explorer
● On

Settings
● On

Documents
● On

Downloads
○ Off

Music
● On

Pictures
○ Off

Don't forget

If you find that you do not use some items very much once they have been added to the Start menu, they can be removed by dragging their buttons **Off** in Step 5.

6 The items selected in Step 5 appear on the Start menu, above the Power button

A≣	Access 2016
	Acer ⌄
	Adobe Design Premium CS5 ⌄
Ⓐ	Adobe Download Assistant
	Adobe Photoshop Elements 15
	Adobe Reader XI
⊘	Alarms & Clock
	B

🔍 Type here to search

Working with Groups

By default, the apps on the Start menu are arranged in groups, such as Everyday apps. However, apps can be arranged into other groups, and new ones can also be created, by dragging apps between groups. To do this:

 Click and hold on a tile and drag it into another group to place it here. If there is no space, the other apps will move to accommodate the new one

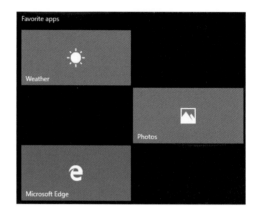

If a group is moved on the Start menu, its name moves with it.

 Drag the tile into an empty space to create a new group

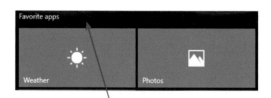

Depending on your geographic location, some terms will appear with alternative spellings; e.g. Customize/ Customise, Personalize/ Personalise.

 Click and drag on the title bar of a group to move the whole group

Naming groups

In their initial state, groups on the Start menu are either not named or they have a default name, but it is possible to give them all their own individual names or titles. To do this:

 Move the cursor over the top of a group and click on the current name or on this button at the right-hand side

Everyday apps

2 Double-click on the current name

Everyday apps

3 Enter a new name for the group

My best apps

4 The name is applied at the top of the group

My best apps

Weather

Photos

Groove Music

Microsoft Edge

Money

Fri 21

Mail

Maps

Hot tip

Group names can be edited using the same process as when creating them in the first place.

Resizing Tiles

As well as rearranging tiles, their sizes can also be edited on the Start menu. Depending on the specific Windows app, there may be up to four options for resizing tiles in Windows 10 – Small, Medium, Wide, and Large, with the initial selection made for you:

Some apps only have options for Small or Medium sizes.

 Right-click on a tile to select it, and click on the **Resize** button from the context menu that appears

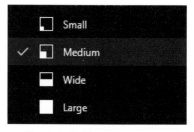

	Unpin from Start
	Resize >
	More >

 The current size of the tile is shown with a tick next to it

	Small	
✓	Medium	
	Wide	
	Large	

34

 Click on another option to resize the tile

✓	Small	
	Medium	
	Wide	
	Large	

The **Large** size is a good option for a tile that can then be used as a Live Tile, to display its contents or real-time information (see page 89).

 If the size is made smaller, the tile is reduced in size and a gap appears around it (unless there is another tile small enough to fill the space next to it)

 For a wide tile, there will be options for making it **Large**, **Medium** or **Small**

Creating Folders

Tiles can be pinned to the Start menu (see page 82), which means that over time it can begin to appear a bit cluttered, with dozens of tiles competing for space. To help organize the Start menu, there is an option for creating folders, so that similar apps can be grouped together within the one tile. To do this:

1 Drag one tile over another to create the group. Ideally, the tiles should be for similar types of apps; e.g. for entertainment

2 The two apps are displayed in the newly created folder

3 Click on a folder to view its contents. Click on this button to minimize the folder again

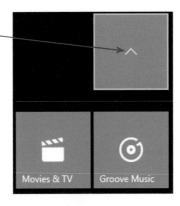

4 To remove an app from a folder, open the folder and drag the app out of the folder and back onto the Start menu

The Desktop and Taskbar

The Desktop is an integral part of Windows, and when you boot up Windows 10 it opens at the Desktop. This also displays the Taskbar at the bottom of the screen:

The Desktop can also be accessed by pressing **WinKey** + **D** or by right-clicking on the Start button and selecting **Desktop**.

Shortcut icons   Search box   Desktop background

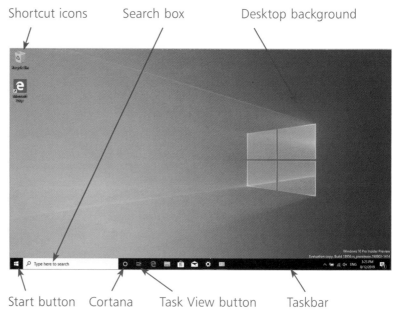

If an app has two or more windows open, each of them will be displayed when you move the cursor over the app's icon on the Taskbar.

Start button   Cortana   Task View button   Taskbar

 1   Move the cursor over items on the Taskbar to see open windows for that item. Click on a window to make that the active one

You can customize the Notification area by right-clicking on an empty area on the Taskbar, clicking on **Taskbar settings** and then clicking **Select which icons appear on the taskbar** underneath the **Notification area** sub-heading.

 2   The Notification area at the right-hand side of the Taskbar has speaker, network and other system tools. Click on one to see more information about that item

Shutting Down

Options for shutting down Windows have been amended with some versions of the operating system. In the Windows 10 November 2019 Update, this functionality can be accessed from the Start menu.

Shutting down from the Start menu

 Click on the **Start** button

 Right-click on the **Power** button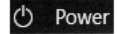

 Click on either the **Sleep**, **Shut down** or **Restart** buttons; or

For some updates to Windows, you will need to restart your computer for them to take effect.

4 Right-click on the **Start** button and select either **Sign out**, **Sleep**, **Shut down** or **Restart** from the **Shut down or sign out** option

File Explorer	Sign out
Search	Sleep
Run	Shut down
Shut down or sign out　　〉	Restart

Task View and Timeline

A useful feature in Windows 10 is the Task View option. This is located on the Taskbar and can be used to view all open apps and also add new desktops. To use Task View:

 Click on this button on the Taskbar

 To show or hide the Task View button, right-click on the button and check On or Off the **Show Task View button** option

Apps can only be open on one desktop at a time. So, if an app is open on one desktop and you try to open it on another, you will be taken to the desktop with the already open app. For adding additional desktops, see the next page.

38

 The Task View displays minimized versions of the currently open apps and windows

 As more windows are opened, the format is arranged accordingly

Although the shortcuts and background are the same for each desktop, the Taskbar will change depending on the open apps.

5 If an app has more than one window open (e.g. File Explorer), each window is displayed within Task View

6 Click on a window in Task View to make it the active window

Adding Desktops

Another function within Task View is for creating additional desktops. This can be useful if you want to separate different categories of tasks on your computer. For instance, you may want to keep your open entertainment apps on a different desktop to your productivity ones. To create additional desktops:

 Click on the **Task View** button on the Taskbar

 The current desktop is displayed with the open windows

3 Click on the **New desktop** button

4 The new desktop is displayed at the top of the Task View window

5 Click on the new desktop to access it. Each desktop has the same background and shortcuts

6 Open apps on the new desktop. These will be separate from the apps on any other desktop

Beware

If you add too many desktops it may become confusing in terms of the content on each one.

Don't forget

The default names of different desktops cannot be changed; i.e. they are Desktop 1, Desktop 2, etc.

Hot tip

To delete a desktop, click on the Task View button and click on the cross that appears when you hover your mouse over the desktop you want to remove.

Don't forget

Click on the **Task View** button to move between desktops.

39

...cont'd

Timeline

Another feature within Task View is the Timeline. This displays a chronological list of items, that you have accessed on your PC over the past 30 days. The Timeline enables you to return to items that were viewed or edited on a specific date, and you can then carry on working on them without having to search for them within their parent app or File Explorer. To use the Timeline:

 Open Task View as shown on page 38. Drag on the sidebar to move through dates when you worked on items on your PC, or scroll down the page

 The content is displayed for each date. Click on an item to access it within its own app

Adding a Phone

The Timeline can also be used to display web pages that are open on a smartphone that has been linked to your Windows 10 PC. To do this, the phone has to first be added to the PC:

1 Open the Settings app and click on the **Phone** option

	Phone
	Link your Android, iPhone

2 Click on the **Add a phone** button

Add a phone

3 Select your type of smartphone and click on the **Continue** button

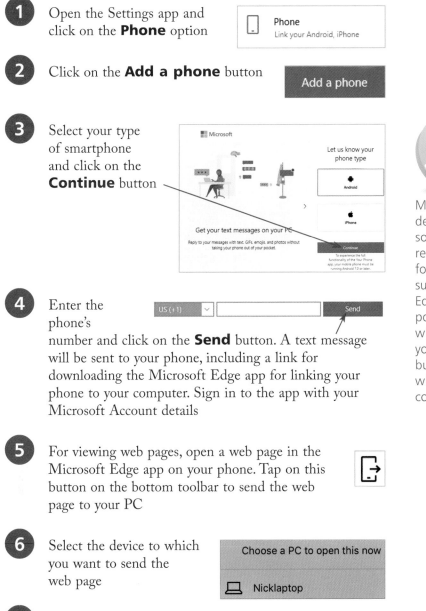

Microsoft

Let us know your phone type

Android

iPhone

Get your text messages on your PC

Reply to your messages with text, GIFs, emojis, and photos without taking your phone out of your pocket.

Continue

To experience the full functionality of the Your Phone app, your mobile phone must be running Android 7.0 or later.

4 Enter the phone's

US (+1)   ⌄   [   ]   Send

number and click on the **Send** button. A text message will be sent to your phone, including a link for downloading the Microsoft Edge app for linking your phone to your computer. Sign in to the app with your Microsoft Account details

5 For viewing web pages, open a web page in the Microsoft Edge app on your phone. Tap on this button on the bottom toolbar to send the web page to your PC

6 Select the device to which you want to send the web page

Choose a PC to open this now

🖥 Nicklaptop

7 The web page opens in the Microsoft Edge app on your Windows 10 PC. It can also be viewed in the Timeline when Task View is accessed

Beware

Microsoft Account details are required so that the app can recognize the linked PC for the phone. For apps such as the Microsoft Edge browser, it is possible to use the app without signing in with your Microsoft Account, but this means that you will not be able to share content to your PC.

Click on a notification to open it and view its full contents.

Don't forget

Notifications for certain apps also appear on screen for a short period of time in a small banner, to alert you to the fact that there is a new notification.

42

The screen brightness can be adjusted directly from the Action Center button on the Taskbar. To do this, click on the Action Center button and drag the **Brightness** slider accordingly. This is a new feature in the Windows 10 November 2019 Update.

Notifications

In the modern digital world there is an increasing desire to keep updated about what is happening in our online world. With Windows 10, the Action Center (which contains the Notification area) can be used to display information from a variety of sources, so that you never miss an update or a notification from one of your apps. To view your notifications:

 Click on the **Action Center** button on the far right of the Taskbar

 New notifications appear at the top of the panel. For selecting what appears, see the next page

 Quick action buttons appear at the bottom of the panel. Click on an item to activate or deactivate it (when a button is blue, the item is active)

Settings for notifications

To change settings for the Action Center:

 Click on the **Settings** app and access **System** > **Notifications & actions**

System
☐ Display
◁») Sound
☐ Notifications & actions

Hot tip

If notification icons are added to the Taskbar, their options can be selected by right-clicking on them.

 Under the **Quick actions** heading, click on the **Edit your quick actions** option

Quick actions
You can add, remove, or rearrange your quick actions directly in action center.
Edit your quick actions

3 Click on this button next to one of the Quick actions items to remove it from the Quick actions panel

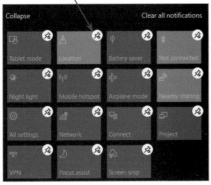

Hot tip

Notifications can also be shown on the Lock screen by dragging the **Show notifications on the lock screen** button **On** in the **Notifications & actions** settings.

☑ Show notifications on the lock screen

4 Under the **Get notifications from these senders** heading, drag the buttons **On** or **Off** to specify the items that appear in the Action Center. For instance, if the **Mail** button is **On**, you will be notified whenever you receive a new email

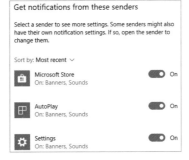

43

Focus Assist

Notifications can be an excellent way to ensure that you never miss an important message or update. However, if there are too many notifications, or they are appearing too frequently, it can become annoying if you are trying to concentrate on something else on your PC. To combat this, there are options for specifying how you want to receive notifications and how often. This is known as Focus assist, and it can be managed within the Settings app:

1 Open the Settings app and click on the **Focus assist** button within the **System** section

Don't forget

Notifications appear in their own panel on the screen and also in the Action Center. If Focus assist is used to restrict notifications from appearing, they will still be available in the Action Center.

2 Check **On** the **Priority only** radio button to control which notifications appear on your PC. Click on the **Customize your priority list** link

3 Check **On** or **Off** the options for notifications that come from a linked phone. This can be done for calls, texts and reminders

Hot tip

For details about how to pin contacts to the Taskbar, see page 203.

4 Check **On** the **Show notifications from pinned contacts on taskbar** checkbox to see these. Click on the **Add contacts** button to allow notifications from specific contacts

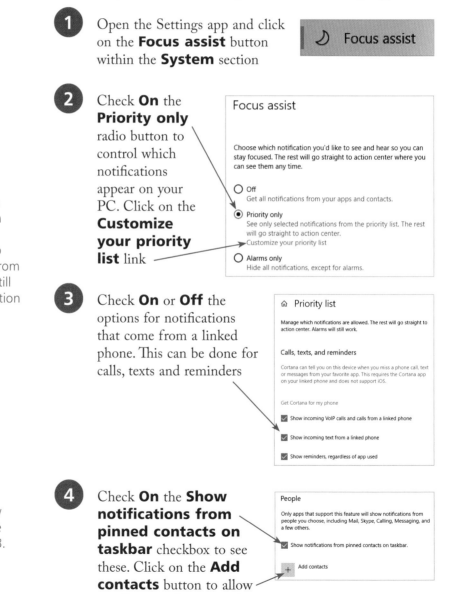

Focus assist

Focus assist

Choose which notification you'd like to see and hear so you can stay focused. The rest will go straight to action center where you can see them any time.

○ Off
Get all notifications from your apps and contacts.

◉ Priority only
See only selected notifications from the priority list. The rest will go straight to action center.
Customize your priority list

○ Alarms only
Hide all notifications, except for alarms.

⌂ Priority list

Manage which notifications are allowed. The rest will go straight to action center. Alarms will still work.

Calls, texts, and reminders

Cortana can tell you on this device when you miss a phone call, text or messages from your favorite app. This requires the Cortana app on your linked phone and does not support iOS.

Get Cortana for my phone

☑ Show incoming VoIP calls and calls from a linked phone

☑ Show incoming text from a linked phone

☑ Show reminders, regardless of app used

People

Only apps that support this feature will show notifications from people you choose, including Mail, Skype, Calling, Messaging, and a few others.

☑ Show notifications from pinned contacts on taskbar

+ Add contacts

5 On the main Focus assist page, drag the buttons **On** or **Off** for specifying automatic rules for when notifications are displayed; e.g. during certain times or if you are playing a game

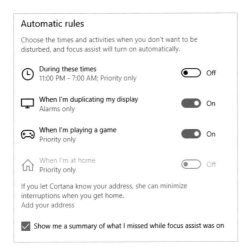

Click on each item in Step 5 to access options for specifying when notifications can be received, as in Step 6.

6 Click on the **During these times** option and specify times during which you do not want to receive any notifications

Settings

Accessing Settings

The Settings in Windows 10 provide options for how you set up your computer and how it operates. There are 13 main categories of Settings, each of which has a number of sub-categories. The Settings app can be accessed in a number of ways:

Some of the Settings have been updated in the Windows 10 November 2019 Update.

1 Click on the **Start** button

2 Click on the **Settings** button on the Start menu or the **Settings** tile on the Start menu, or

1 Click on the **Action Center** button on the Taskbar

2 Click on the **All settings** button, or

1 Enter **Settings** into the **Search** box (see page 62) and click on the **Settings** button

2 In the **Settings** app, click on one of the main categories to view the options within that category

Add the **Settings** app to the Taskbar for quick access. To do this, access it from the Start menu, right-click on it and click on **More** > **Pin to taskbar**.

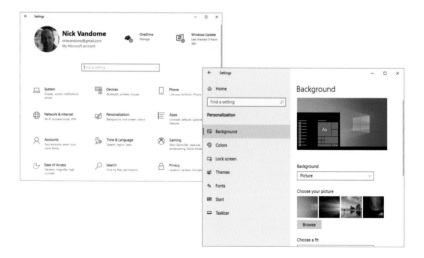

System Settings

The System Settings provide numerous options to specify how your computer looks and operates. They include:

- **Display**. This contains options for changing the size of items on the screen, the orientation of the screen, and options for adjusting the screen brightness, either manually or automatically.

The **Night light** feature in the **Display** setting can be used to apply a warmer color for the computer's display to create a more restful environment, particularly at night time. Click on the **Night light settings** link to apply these settings.

47

- **Sound**. This contains options for selecting output and input devices for the sound on your PC, and for setting the volume.

- **Notifications & actions**. This contains options for selecting which notification icons appear on the Taskbar, and specifying which apps can be used to display notifications; e.g. your calendar and email.

- **Focus assist**. This can be used to determine how notifications operate. See pages 44-45.

- **Power & sleep**. This contains options for when the screen is turned off when not being used, and when the computer goes to sleep when it is not being used. This ranges from one minute to never.

...cont'd

- **Battery**. This can be used on laptops, and displays the charge level of the battery and what is using the battery most. It also has options for saving battery power.

- **Storage**. This displays how much storage has been taken up on your computer and has options for where you want to save certain types of content. This can be the PC or an external drive, such as a hard drive or a USB flashdrive.

- **Tablet mode**. This can be used on desktop and laptop computers, using a mouse and keyboard to replicate the operation of using a touchscreen device or tablet with Windows 10. This includes expanding the Start menu to full screen.

- **Multitasking**. This contains options for working with windows and desktops. In the **Snap** section you can turn on options for arranging windows when they are moved to the edge of the screen, and in the **Virtual desktops** section you can specify whether the Taskbar (and Alt + Tab) shows all open windows, or just those for the current desktop.

- **Projecting to this PC**. This can be used to allow other Windows 10 devices (computers, tablets or phones) to project their screens onto your computer so that you can view the screen and also interact with it.

- **Shared experiences**. This can be used for sharing content between computers, including the Nearby sharing feature. See pages 212-213 for details.

- **Clipboard**. This has options for saving multiple items to the clipboard, and viewing them across different devices.

- **Remote Desktop**. This contains options for controlling your PC from a remote device, with an appropriate app.

- **About**. This contains information about your computer and the version of Windows that you are using.

Devices Settings

The Devices Settings provide settings for how the hardware connected with your computer operates. They include:

- **Bluetooth & other devices**. This can be used to link your computer to compatible Bluetooth devices, so that they can share content over short distances with radiowaves. The two devices have to be "paired" initially to be able to share content.

- **Printers & scanners**. This can be used to add new printers or scanners to your computer. These can either be wireless ones, or ones that connect via cable. In most cases, the required software will be installed with Windows 10, or if not, it will be downloaded from the internet.

- **Mouse**. This contains options for customizing the mouse. These include setting the main button (Left, by default) and how the scrolling operates with the mouse, such as the number of lines that can be scrolled at a time (Multiple, by default).

- **Touchpad**. This contains options for customizing the touchpad (for a laptop).

- **Typing**. This contains options for correcting your typing as you go. These include autocorrecting misspelled words, and highlighting misspelled words.

- **Pen & Windows Ink**. This contains options for using a stylus to jot down notes, and sketch on the screen.

- **AutoPlay**. This contains options for applying AutoPlay for external devices such as removable drives and memory cards. If AutoPlay is On, the devices will be activated and accessed when they are attached to your computer.

- **USB**. This can be used to flag up any issues with connected USB devices.

Printers can also be added through the **Control Panel**. This is done in the **Devices and Printers** section, under **Hardware and Sound**. Click on the **Add a printer** button and follow the wizard.

The Phone Setting can be used to link your PC and your smartphone, so that tasks can be started on one device and then continued on another. See page 41 for details.

49

...cont'd

Network & Internet Settings

The Network & Internet Settings provide settings related to connecting to networks, usually for accessing the internet. They include:

- **Status**. This displays the current Wi-Fi status; i.e. whether the computer is connected to the internet or not.

- **Wi-Fi**. This contains options for connecting to the internet via your Wi-Fi router (or public hotspots). There is also an option for managing your Wi-Fi networks.

- **Ethernet**. This can be used if you are connecting to the internet with an Ethernet cable. This connects to the Ethernet port on your computer, and internet access is delivered through the use of your telephone line.

- **Dial-up**. This can be used if you have a dial-up modem for connecting to the internet. This is not common these days, but is still a valid means of internet access.

- **VPN**. This can be used to connect to a corporate network over VPN (Virtual Private Network). If you are doing this, you will need certain settings and details from your network administrator.

- **Airplane mode**. This can be used to turn off wireless communication when you are on a plane, so that you can still use your computer (laptop) safely.

- **Mobile hotspot**. This can be used to determine how the computer interacts with mobile hotspots for connecting to shared public networks.

- **Proxy**. This contains options for using a proxy server for Ethernet or Wi-Fi connections.

Don't forget

If Wi-Fi is turned **On** in the Wi-Fi settings, any routers in range should be recognized. A password will probably then be required to connect to the router.

Personalization Settings

The Personalization Settings provide options for customizing the look and feel of Windows 10. They include:

- **Background**. This can be used to change the Desktop background in Windows 10. You can select images from the pictures provided, solid colors, a slideshow, or your own photos (using the **Browse** button). You can also choose how the background fits the screen (the default is Fill).

- **Colors**. This contains options for selecting a color for borders, buttons, the Taskbar and the Start menu background.

- **Lock screen**. This can be used to select a background for the Lock screen. You can use the images provided and also select your own photos (using the **Browse** button). You can also select apps that display relevant information on the Lock screen, such as email notifications or calendar events.

Hot tip

In the Colors section there is also an option for making the Start menu, Taskbar and Action Center (Notifications) transparent.

- **Themes**. This contains options for color themes that can be applied for several elements within the Windows 10 interface.

- **Fonts**. This displays the available fonts on your system and enables you to change their size.

- **Start**. This contains options for how the Start menu operates. It can be used to view the Start menu in full screen mode and also display recently used items in the Start menu.

- **Taskbar**. This contains options for locking the Taskbar, automatically hiding it, changing the icon size, and specifying its screen location (left, top, right or bottom).

...cont'd

Apps Settings

The Apps Settings provide options for specifying how apps work and interact with Windows 10. They include:

- **Apps & features**. This contains information about the apps that you have on your computer. This includes their size and installation date. There is

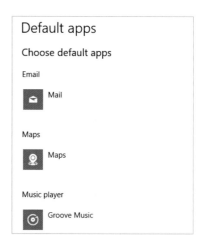

also an option to specify how apps can be downloaded to your computer. Click on the **Choose where to get apps** drop-down box and select one of the options (**The Microsoft Store only (recommended)** is the most secure option).

- **Default apps**. This can be used to select default apps for opening certain items such as email, music, photos and videos. Click on each app to select another default app, or to look for one in the Microsoft Store.

- **Offline maps**. This contains options for downloading maps so that you can use them even when you are offline. There is also an option for only downloading maps when you are connected to Wi-Fi, to save any unwanted charges if you have a mobile data plan.

- **Apps for websites**. This can be used to allow compatible apps to open websites, rather than using a browser.

- **Video playback**. This can be used to change the video settings for video playback apps.

- **Startup**. This can be used to specify apps that start when you log in to your Windows 10 account.

Accounts Settings

The Accounts Settings provide options for adding new online accounts (such as a new email account, or an online storage and sharing service such as Dropbox). They include:

- **Your info**. This displays information about your current account, which will either be the one you signed in to using your Microsoft Account details, or a Local account, which has no online presence. 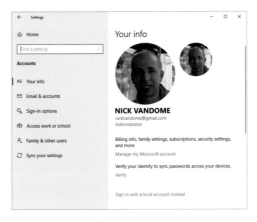 You can also swap between accounts here.

The Accounts Settings can be used to switch between a Microsoft Account and a Local account for signing in to your PC.

- **Email & accounts**. This can be used to add email accounts and also add a Microsoft Account.

- **Sign-in options**. This contains security options for signing in to your account. You can create a PIN, Password or Picture password. Whichever method you choose, this will be required when you sign in to your account from the Lock screen.

- **Access work or school**. This can be used to connect to a workplace network, where you can share certain items. To do this you will need to contact the network administrator in order to obtain the correct settings to connect to the network.

- **Family & other users**. This can be used to set up accounts on your computer for other family members, or friends. They will be able to set their own sign-in options, and you will be able to switch users by clicking on the Start button and then clicking on the icon of the current user.

- **Sync your settings**. This can be used to sync the settings you have on your computer with any other Windows 10 devices that you have. For instance, if you have a desktop computer using Windows 10, you will be able to sync settings and apps with another Windows 10 device, such as a Surface tablet.

53

...cont'd

Time & Language Settings

The Time & Language Settings provide options for the time zone used by your computer, and the format for these items. They include:

● **Date & time**. This can be used to set the date and time, either manually or automatically, using the **Time zone** drop-down menu. There is also a link to **Related settings** in the Control Panel, where formatting options can be applied.

● **Region** and **Language**. These two options can be used to select the language that is used by your computer; e.g. English (United States). You can also add new languages.

The date and time can also be set within the **Clock and Region** section of the Control Panel, under the **Date and Time** heading.

● **Speech**. This contains options for how the speech function operates when using Windows 10. This includes the language to use when you are using speech, and also the default voice if using apps that speak text from the screen.

Gaming Settings

The Gaming Settings contain a range of options:

- **Xbox Game Bar**. This can be used for settings for the Game Bar controller that can accessed when playing games with Windows 10.

The Game Bar can be opened with keyboard shortcuts (**WinKey** + **G** by default), and it can be used to capture screenshots or video recordings of the games being played. These can then be shared with other games.

- **Captures**. This contains options for capturing screenshots of games being played and game clips.

- **Game Mode**. This ensures the best possible gaming experience with Windows 10. Drag the **Use Game Mode** button **On** to activate it.

- **Xbox Networking**. This contains information about the network to which your Xbox is connected.

Don't forget

For more information about using the Xbox Console app and playing games with Windows 10, see pages 179-180.

The Vision Settings are: Display, Mouse pointer, Text cursor, Magnifier, Color filters, High contrast, and Narrator. The Hearing Settings are: Audio and Closed captions. The Interaction Settings are: Speech, Keyboard, Mouse, and Eye Control.

The Display Settings include an option to **Make text bigger**. This is done by dragging a slider to specify the size of text throughout Windows 10. This is a new feature in the Windows 10 November 2019 Update.

Make text bigger

Sample text

Drag the slider until the sample text is easy to read, then click Apply

A ——————●———————— A

Apply

...cont'd

Ease of Access Settings

The Ease of Access Settings are divided into three sections, for Vision, Hearing and Interaction. They include:

- **Display**. This contains options for changing the size of everything on the screen and adjusting the brightness.

- **Mouse pointer**. This has options for changing size and color of the onscreen mouse pointer.

- **Text cursor**. This has options for changing the size and color of the text cursor.

- **Magnifier**. This can be used to magnify what is being viewed on the screen, by up to 1600% of the standard view.

- **Color filters**. This can be used to apply color filters to the screen, to make photos and colors easier to see.

- **High contrast**. This contains options for applying high contrast themes for Windows 10, to make certain elements more pronounced. This can be useful for users with dyslexia.

- **Narrator**. This can be used to activate a screen reader so text, buttons and toolbars can be read out loud. A voice style can be selected, along with the speed and pitch of reading.

- **Audio**. This can be used to change the device's volume, turn on mono audio, and display audio alerts visually.

- **Closed captions**. This can be used by hearing-impaired users to access and customize text subtitles for items such as movies or multimedia content.

- **Speech**. This contains options for using voice dictation instead of using the keyboard for text entry.

- **Keyboard**. This can be used to enable the onscreen keyboard, and options for keyboard shortcuts and keyboard sounds for when certain keys are pressed.

- **Mouse**. This contains an option for using the numeric keypad for controlling the mouse pointer.

- **Eye control**. This is an option for using eye control devices for entering content with a mouse and keyboard.

Search Settings

The Search Settings can be used to set certain permissions for search criteria and also general options for searching for items on your computer and on the web. They include:

- **Permissions & History**. This contains options for the type of content that is allowed to be viewed when searching on the web. The options are **Strict**, which filters out adult content; **Moderate**, which filters adult images and videos, but not text; and **Off**, which does not filter adult content. There are also options for searching the accounts on your computer.

The separate Search Settings is a new feature in the Windows 10 November 2019 Update.

Permissions & History

SafeSearch

In Windows Search, web previews will not automatically load web results if they may contain adult content. If you choose to preview web results, we'll apply the setting below.

- ⦿ Strict - Filter out adult text, images, and videos from my web results
- ◯ Moderate - Filter adult images and videos but not text from my web results
- ◯ Off - Don't filter adult content from my web results

Cloud content search

Search your content from cloud services such as OneDrive and Outlook.

Microsoft account
Search your personal emails, photos, documents, and files.
◼️◯ On

Work or School account
Search your work or school emails, documents, files, and people.
◼️◯ On

- **Searching Windows**. This can be used to specify which areas of your computer are searched. This can be either your libraries and the desktop, or your entire computer. Specific folders can also be added, or excluded, from the locations to be searched.

...cont'd

Privacy Settings

The Privacy Settings include general privacy options such as how apps and websites make contact with your device. The Privacy Settings can also be used to allow or deny certain apps access to your device's location They include:

● **General**. This contains settings for general privacy options, including letting apps make advertising more specific to you, based on app usage, letting websites provide locally relevant content and letting Windows track app launches. There are also links to a range of information about privacy options, including a Privacy dashboard of items and a Privacy statement.

● **Speech**. This can be used to train Windows and the personal digital assistant, Cortana, to your speaking styles, so that they can operate more efficiently.

● **Inking & typing personalization**. This can be used to create a personal dictionary based on your typing (and handwriting if used) patterns.

● **Diagnostics & feedback**. This contains options for how feedback is sent to Microsoft.

- **Activity history**. This contains options for how Microsoft can collect information from the activities on your PC.

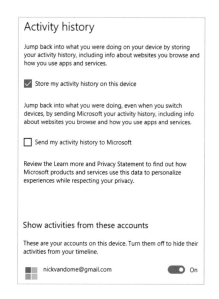

- **Location**. This can be used to turn On or Off the location services, to allow or deny apps the use of your location.

- **Notifications**. This can be used to specify which apps can access notifications in the Action Center and the Lock screen.

- **Account info**. This can be used to allow apps access to your name, picture and account info.

- **Tasks**. This can be used to specify which apps can access certain tasks being performed on your computer.

- The following options can be used to allow or deny apps access to these specific functions: **Camera**, **Microphone**, **Contacts**, **Calendar**, **Call history**, **Email**, **Messaging**, and **Radios**. There are also options for allowing access to **Automatic file downloads**, **Documents**, **Pictures**, **Videos**, and **File system**.

- **Other devices**. This can be used to view external devices, such as an Xbox, that have access to your apps.

- **Background apps**. This can be used to specify which apps can receive notifications and updates even when not in use.

The more access you give in terms of your own information and allowing apps to share your location, the more unwanted information you may be sent.

...cont'd

Update & Security Settings

The Update & Security Settings provide options for installing updates to Windows, and also backing up and recovering the data on your computer. They include:

- **Windows Update**. This can be used to install system updates, such as those to Windows 10, and also important security updates. They can be set to be checked for and installed automatically (using the **Advanced options** button) or manually (using the **Check for updates** button). For some updates, your computer will shut down and restart automatically.

Don't forget

Because of the nature of Windows 10 – e.g. it is designed as an online service – there will be regular updates. Check the Windows Update section regularly, even if you have set updates to be installed automatically, as you will be able to view the details of installed updates.

- **Delivery Optimization**. This has options for using apps, and other downloads, from other computers using the same Microsoft Account.

- **Windows Security**. This contains a range of options for protecting your computer including protection against viruses, account protection, and a firewall and network protection.

...cont'd

- **Backup**. This can be used to back up your important files and documents. It is best if this is done to an external hard drive that is kept separately from your computer. Connect an external hard drive and click on the **Add a drive** button to start the process.

- **Troubleshoot**. This contains options for troubleshooting problems with Windows 10 or your PC. Select an option and click on the **Run the troubleshooter** button.

- **Recovery**. This can be used if you encounter problems with the way that Windows 10 is operating. You can select to refresh your computer 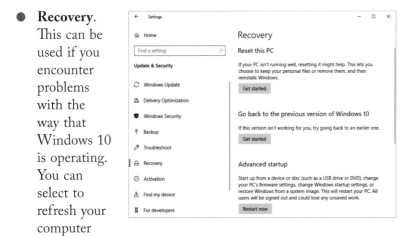 and keep all of your files intact (although they should always be backed up first); reinstall Windows completely, which will reset it completely and you will lose all of your files and any apps you have downloaded; or return to an earlier version of Windows that was on your computer, without losing any files.

- **Activation**. This can be used to activate your copy of Windows 10, to confirm that it is an authorized version. Activation can be done online.

- **Find my device**. This can be used to set up Find My Device for locating a lost device, via the website at: **account.microsoft.com/devices**

- **For developers**. This contains options for advanced users involved in programming and app development.

- **Windows Insider Program**. This can be used to gain access to the Insider Program, for downloading preview versions of the latest Windows 10 updates.

61

Searching

Searching for items and information on computers and the internet has come a long way since the first search engines on the web. Most computer operating systems now have sophisticated search facilities for finding things on your own computer as well as searching over the web. They also now have personal digital assistants, which are voice-activated search functions that can be used instead of typing search requests.

Windows 10 has a Search box built in to the Taskbar. Separate searches can be performed with Cortana, the digital voice assistant (see pages 64-67).

Using the Search box for text searching

To use the Search box for text-only searches, over either your computer or the web:

Hot tip

If the Search box is not showing, right-click the on the Taskbar, then click **Search** > **Show search box**.

Hot tip

The top search result is displayed at the top of the window in Step 3.

Hot tip

Click on the buttons at the top of the Search window to specify locations over which the search will be performed. These are **All**, **Apps**, **Documents**, **Email**, **Web** and **More**.

1 Click in the Search box

2 Enter a search term (or website address)

3 Click on one of the results, or on one of the **See web results** buttons, to view the search results page in the Microsoft Edge browser

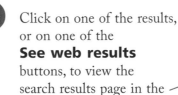

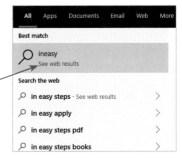

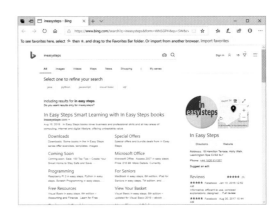

Asking a question

The Search box can also be used to ask specific questions:

1 Enter a question in the Search box

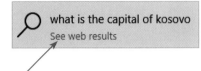

what is the capital of kosovo
See web results

2 Click on the **See web results** button at the top of the Search box to view the results in the Microsoft Edge browser (in some instances, the answer will be displayed at the top of the Search box too)

The magnifying glass icon indicates that a search is going to be undertaken on the web, and this will be displayed on a search results page, as in Step 2.

63

Searching over your computer

As well as searching over the web, the Search box can also be used to find items on your computer:

1 Enter a search query into the Search box and click on one of the options on the top toolbar to search for items from that location on your computer; e.g. Documents. Click on one of the results to open the item on your computer

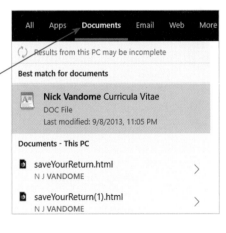

If you are searching for a keyword over files on your computer, the search will be conducted over the text in documents and folders, not just the document titles. It will also search over the online backup and storage facility, OneDrive, if you have this set up (see pages 166-169).

Setting Up Cortana

To ensure that you can use Cortana to perform voice searches and queries, the language settings on your Windows 10 computer have to be set up correctly. To do this:

The county or region, display language and speech language should be the same in order for Cortana to work.

1 Open the **Settings** app and click on the **Time & Language** button

> Time & Language
> Speech, region, date

2 Click on the **Region** button

> 🌐 Region

3 Click here to select a country or region

> Region
>
> Country or region
>
> United States ⌄
>
> Windows and apps might use your country or region to give you local content.
>
> Regional format
>
> Current format: English (United States)
>
> Recommended [English (United States)] ⌄
>
> Windows formats dates and times based on your language and regional preferences.
>
> Regional format data
>
> Select Change data formats to switch among calendars, date, and time formats supported by the region.

4 Select a **Regional format**, which should match the region in Step 3

If the Cortana button is not displayed once the languages have been set, right-click on the Cortana icon on the Taskbar, then check **On** the **Show Cortana button** option.

5 Click on the **Speech** button under **Time & Language**

> 🎤 Speech

6 Select the same **Speech language** as the one used as the display language in Step 4

> Speech language
>
> Choose the language you speak with your device
>
> English (United States) ⌄

Using Cortana

Voice searching with Cortana

As with text searches, Cortana can be used to search over various places and for different items:

1 Click on the Microphone button to

Ask Cortana

the right of the Cortana box to begin a voice search

2 This symbol is displayed in the Search window to indicate that Cortana is listening

3 Cortana can be used for a wide range of general requests, which display the results from the web; e.g. ask about the capital city of a country and click on the result to see more details on the web

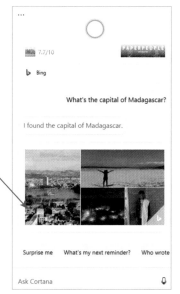

4 Queries can also be made in relation to the web; e.g. opening a specific website. Cortana can also be used to display specific information from the web, such as a weather forecast or sports results

Having the Cortana button separated from the Search box is a new feature in the Windows 10 November 2019 Update.

Hot tip

Cortana can be used directly from the Lock screen, to ask general queries, such as "What is the weather in my area?" or to play a song from the Groove Music app.

...cont'd

The Cortana interface has been updated in the Windows 10 November 2019 Update.

Don't forget

Cortana voice commands can be used to turn Off, Restart or put your PC to Sleep. They can also be used to change the system volume. Also, an increasing range of apps support Cortana, so can be used in conjunction with it; e.g. for playing movies with Netflix.

5 If the query is general – e.g. "**Open Microsoft**" – various options in terms of apps from your computer will be displayed. Click on one of the apps to open it directly from Cortana

←

◯

Which Microsoft do you want?

🃏 Microsoft Solitaire Collection Preview

🌐 Microsoft Wi-Fi

🃏 Microsoft Solitaire Collection

e Microsoft Edge

🏬 Microsoft Store

🗔 Microsoft News

 6 Cortana can be used to open specific apps; e.g. by saying "**Open Mail**". If required, options will be available, depending on the request. Click on an item to access it

Open mail.

OK.

I'll open Mail...

✉ Mail

Cortana settings

A range of settings can be made for Cortana directly from the Cortana window when a search is being performed:

1 Open Cortana and click on the **Menu** button in the top left-hand corner of the Cortana window

2 Click on the **Settings** button

3 The Cortana settings are displayed

Click on the **Permissions** button in Step 3 to access options for giving Cortana access to other devices; e.g. your computer's microphone.

4 Click on the **Privacy** button in Step 3 to access options for specifying information Cortana can store about you, and how to clear data

5 Click on the **Talking to Cortana** button in Step 3 to access options for using a **Wakeword** for accessing Cortana (e.g. just saying **Cortana**, without having to click on the Cortana icon), and a default method of using Cortana; e.g. **Speak** or **Type**

Adding and Switching Users

If more than one person uses the computer, each person can have a user account defined with a username and a password. To create a new user account, as either a Microsoft Account or a Local account:

1 Access the **Settings** app and select **Accounts**

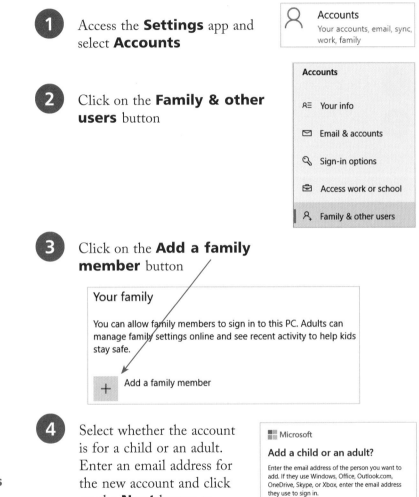

2 Click on the **Family & other users** button

The email address is a required field when creating a new user with a Microsoft Account.

3 Click on the **Add a family member** button

Your family

You can allow family members to sign in to this PC. Adults can manage family settings online and see recent activity to help kids stay safe.

+ Add a family member

At Step 3 there is also an option to **Add someone else to this PC**, not just a family member.

4 Select whether the account is for a child or an adult. Enter an email address for the new account and click on the **Next** button to access a window for adding a password. Then, click on the **Next** button in Step 6. If the user does not have an email address, click the **The person I want to add doesn't have an email address** link, and follow Step 5

Microsoft

Add a child or an adult?

Enter the email address of the person you want to add. If they use Windows, Office, Outlook.com, OneDrive, Skype, or Xbox, enter the email address they use to sign in.

◉ Add a child

Kids are safer online when they have their own account

○ Add an adult

Enter their email address

The person I want to add doesn't have an email address

Cancel   Next

5 Enter an email address for the new user, then click on the **Next** button and add a password

■■ Microsoft

Create account

| New email | @outlook.com ∨ |

Use a phone number instead

Use your email instead

Back   Next

When creating a new account, a phone number can be used to initially set up the account, instead of an email address. A text message is sent to the phone to authenticate it, enabling the account to be signed in to without the need for a password. This is a new feature in the Windows 10 November 2019 Update.

6 Click on the **Next** button to complete the setup wizard

Next

7 The user is added to the Accounts page

Your family

You can allow family members to sign in to this PC. Adults can manage family settings online and see recent activity to help kids stay safe.

+   Add a family member

○ lucyvandome17@gmail.com   Can sign in
   Child

Manage family settings online

Hot tip

Family Safety settings can be applied by clicking on the **Manage family settings online** link on the **Family & other users** page (see Step 7). This takes you to your online Microsoft Account page where settings can be applied for items such as web filtering, time controls, and app restrictions.

8 Click on a user to change the type of their account; e.g. from a Local account to a Microsoft Account, or to delete their account

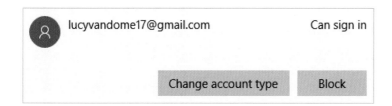

○ lucyvandome17@gmail.com   Can sign in

Change account type   Block

69

...cont'd

Don't forget

When switching users, all of your settings and files are maintained but the new user will not be able to see them, and you will not be able to see theirs when you switch back. Your screen should look exactly the same as you left it.

Beware

If the other accounts have data files open, shutting down without logging them off could cause them to lose information.

Switching users

If you have a number of user accounts defined on the computer (several accounts can be active at the same time), you do not need to close your apps and log off to be able to switch to another user. It is easy to switch back and forth.

 Click on the **Start** button

 Click on your own user account icon and click on another user's name. They will have to enter their own password in order to access their account, at which point they will be signed in. You can then switch between users without each having to log out every time

As an alternative way to switch users:

Press **WinKey** + **L** to lock the current user

Access the sign-in screen for all of the current users and select one as required

Shut down

When you turn off your computer (see page 37), you will be warned if there are other user accounts still logged on to the computer.

 Click on the **Shut down anyway** button to shut down without other users logging off

Someone else is still using this PC. If you shut down now, they could lose unsaved work.

Shut down anyway

3 Working with Apps

"Apps" is now a standard term in computing. Put simply, it is just another name for computer programs. In Windows 10, some apps are preinstalled, while thousands more can be downloaded from the Microsoft Store. This chapter shows how to work with and organize apps in Windows 10, and how to find your way around the Microsoft Store.

72   Starting with Apps

74   Windows 10 Apps

76   Using Windows 10 Apps

78   Classic Apps on the Desktop

79   Closing Apps

80   Viewing All Apps

81   Searching for Apps

82   Pin to Start Menu

83   Pin to Taskbar

84   Using the Microsoft Store

87   Buying Apps

88   Viewing Your Apps

89   Using Live Tiles

90   Install and Uninstall

92   Task Manager

Starting with Apps

The word "app" is now firmly established as a generic term for computer programs on a range of devices. Originally, apps were items that were downloaded to smartphones and tablet computers. However, the terminology has now been expanded to cover any computer program. So, in Windows 10 most programs are referred to as "apps", although some legacy ones may still be referred to as "programs".

There are three clear types of apps within Windows 10:

- **Windows 10 apps**. These are the built-in apps that can be accessed from the Start menu. They cover the areas of communication, entertainment and information, and several of them are linked together through the online sharing service, OneDrive. In Windows 10, they open in their own window on the Desktop, in the same way as the older-style Windows apps (see below).

- **Windows classic apps**. These are the older-style Windows apps that people may be familiar with from previous versions of Windows. These open in the Desktop environment.

- **Microsoft Store apps**. These are apps that can be downloaded from the online Microsoft Store, and cover a wide range of subjects and functionality. Some Microsoft Store apps are free, while others have to be paid for.

Windows 10 apps

Windows 10 apps are accessed from the brightly colored tiles on the Start menu (or listed on the left-hand side). Click on a tile to open the relevant app:

In Windows 10, all apps open directly on the Desktop and their operation is more consistent, regardless of the type of app.

72

...cont'd

Windows classic apps

The Windows classic apps are generally the ones that appeared as default with previous versions of Windows, and would have been accessed from the Start button. The Windows classic apps can be accessed from the Start menu by using the alphabetic list, or searched for via the Taskbar Search box. Windows classic apps have the traditional Windows look and functionality, and they also open on the Desktop.

Some older Windows apps, such as Notepad and Paint, can be found in the Windows Accessories folder in the All apps alphabetic list. Alternatively, they can be searched for using Cortana or the Search box.

73

Microsoft Store apps

The Microsoft Store apps are accessed and downloaded from the online Microsoft Store. Apps can be browsed and searched for in the Store, and when they are downloaded they are added to the All apps alphabetic list on the Start menu.

The Microsoft Store is accessed by clicking on the **Store** tile on the Start menu or on the Taskbar.

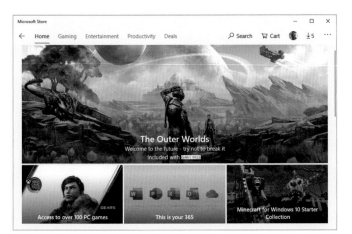

Some of these apps may not be supplied as standard on your Windows 10 system, but you can get them from the Microsoft Store (see pages 84-87).

See Chapter 10 for more information about working with the Calendar, Mail, People and Skype apps, and how content can be shared between the different apps.

There is a significant focus on 3D and Mixed Reality in Windows 10. The **Mixed Reality Portal** app can be used to gain an overview of this technology.

Windows 10 Apps

The Windows 10 apps that are accessed from the All apps alphabetic list on the Start menu cover a range of communication, entertainment and information functions. The apps include:

 3D Viewer. This can be used to download and view 3D objects that have been created by you or other people.

 Alarms & Clock. This provides alarms, clocks for times around the world, a timer and a stopwatch function.

 Calculator. This is a standard calculator that also has an option for using it as a scientific calculator.

 Calendar. This is a calendar that you can use to add appointments and important dates.

 Camera. This can be used to take photos directly onto your computer, but only if it has a built-in camera.

 Groove Music. This can be used to access the online Music Store where music can be downloaded.

 Mail. This is the online Mail facility. You can use it to connect to a selection of email accounts.

 Maps. This provides online access to maps from around the world. It also shows traffic issues.

 Microsoft Edge. This is the default browser in Windows 10 and is covered in detail in Chapter 9.

 Microsoft News. This is one of the information apps that provide real-time news information, based on your location.

 Microsoft Store. This provides access to the online Microsoft Store from where a range of other apps can be bought and downloaded to your computer.

 Mixed Reality Portal. This provides an overview of 3D technology and using it with Windows 10.

 Money. This is one of the information apps that provide real-time financial news, based on your location.

Movies & TV (**Films & TV** in some regions). This is where you will see the movies and TV shows you buy in the Microsoft Store. There is also a link to the Video Store.

 OneDrive. This is an online facility for storing and sharing content from your computer. This includes photos and documents.

 OneNote. This is a Microsoft note-taking app, part of the Office suite of apps.

 Paint 3D. This is an app that can be used to create, view and share 3D objects.

 People. This is the address book app for adding contacts. Your contacts from sites such as Gmail and iCloud can also be imported into the People app.

 Photos. This can be used to view and organize your photos. It can also be used to share and print photos.

 Reader. This can be used to open and view documents in different file formats, such as PDF and TIFF.

 Settings. This can be used to access all of the main settings for customizing and managing Windows 10 and your computer. (See pages 46-61 for details.)

 Snip & Sketch. This can be used to capture and annotate screenshots: an image of the screen being viewed.

 Sports. This is one of the information apps that provide real-time sports news, based on your location.

 Stickies. This is an app for creating short notes that can be "stuck" to the screen, so that they are readily visible.

 Voice Recorder. This can be used to record, save and share audio messages.

 Weather. This provides real-time weather forecasts for locations around the world. By default, it will provide the nearest forecast to your location.

 Xbox Console. This can be used to download and play games, and also play online Xbox games.

A desktop app for OneDrive can also be downloaded from the Microsoft Store. This can be used to view and manage folders and files in OneDrive. The version described on the pages here is the File Explorer version of OneDrive, where the folders and files are displayed in the File Explorer.
App versions of OneDrive can also be downloaded for iOS and Android devices.
OneDrive can also be used to share your content, such as photos and documents, with other people. See pages 166-169 for details.

The information in the Money, News, Sports and Weather apps is provided by Bing.

75

Using Windows 10 Apps

In Windows 8 and 8.1, the newer-style Windows apps had a different look and functionality. However, in Windows 10 all of the apps have been created with a more consistent appearance, although there are still some differences.

Windows 10 apps

Windows 10 apps open in their own window on the Desktop (in Windows 8 and 8.1 they only opened in full screen), and they can be moved and resized in the same way as older-style apps:

 1 Click and drag on the top toolbar to move the app's window

In Windows 10 there has been a conscious effort to achieve a greater consistency between the newer-style apps and the old, classic-style apps.

2 Drag on the bottom or right-hand border to resize the app's window (or the bottom right-hand corner to resize the height and width simultaneously)

...cont'd

Windows 10 app menus
Some Windows 10 apps have their own menus:

1 Click on this button (if available) within the app's window to access its menu

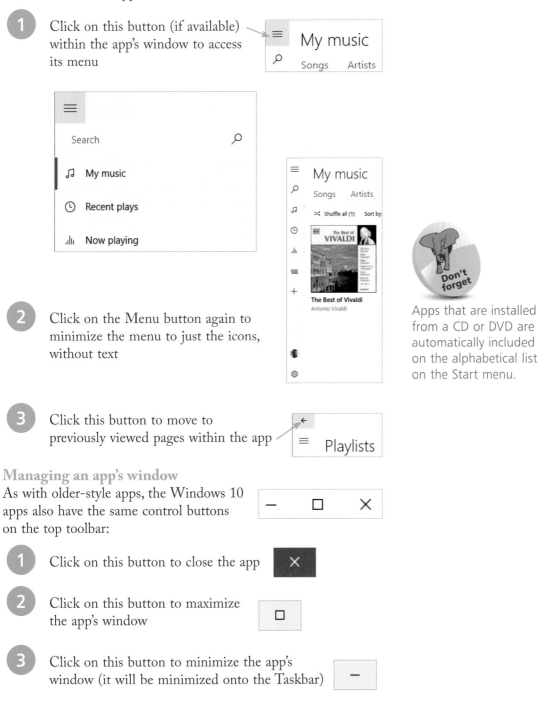

2 Click on the Menu button again to minimize the menu to just the icons, without text

Don't forget

Apps that are installed from a CD or DVD are automatically included on the alphabetical list on the Start menu.

3 Click this button to move to previously viewed pages within the app

Managing an app's window
As with older-style apps, the Windows 10 apps also have the same control buttons on the top toolbar:

1 Click on this button to close the app

2 Click on this button to maximize the app's window

3 Click on this button to minimize the app's window (it will be minimized onto the Taskbar)

Classic Apps on the Desktop

The Windows classic apps open on the Desktop, in the same way as with previous versions of Windows, even though they are opened from the Start menu (or the Taskbar).

Opening a Windows classic app

To open a Windows classic app:

1 Click on the **Start** button and navigate through the app list

2 Select the app you want to open (for example WordPad, from the Windows Accessories section)

3 The app opens on the Desktop

Hot tip

If apps have been pinned to the Taskbar, as shown on page 83, they can be opened directly from there by simply clicking on them.

4 Click on the tabs at the top of the app to access relevant Ribbon toolbars and menus

Closing Apps

There are several ways to close a Windows app:

1 Click on the red **Close** button in the top right of the window

2 Select **File** > **Exit** from the File menu (if available)

3 Press **Alt** + **F4**

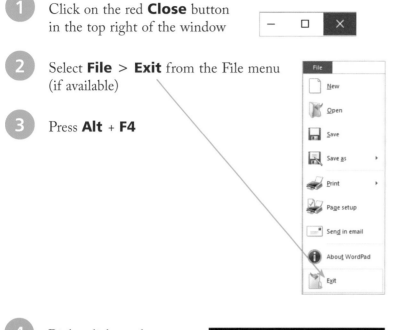

Beware

It is always worth saving a new document as soon as it is created. It should also be saved at regular intervals as you are working on it.

4 Right-click on the icon on the Taskbar and select **Close window** (or **Close all windows** if more than one is open)

	WordPad (2)
	Unpin from taskbar
✕	Close all windows

5 If any changes have been made to the document, you may receive a warning message advising you to save the associated file

WordPad   ✕

Do you want to save changes to Document?

| Save | Don't Save | Cancel |

Viewing All Apps

There is a lot more to Windows 10 than the default Windows 10 apps. Most of the Windows apps that were available with previous versions of Windows are still there, and they are all available directly from the Start button, on the Start menu. To access all of the apps:

1 Click on the **Start** button

2 All of the apps are displayed. Use the scroll bar to move through all of the apps, which are listed alphabetically

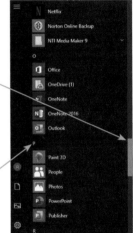

3 Click on a letter heading to view an alphabetic grid for finding apps. Click on a letter to move to that section

The All apps list can be hidden by selecting **Settings** > **Personalization** > **Start**. Drag the **Show app list in Start menu** button **Off**. The apps list is minimized to the side of the screen. Click on this button to maximize the list (the button above it is for viewing the tiles on the Start menu).

Searching for Apps

As you acquire more and more apps, it may become harder to find the ones you want. To help with this, you can use the Search box to search over all of the apps on your computer. To do this:

1 Click in the Search box on the Taskbar

Type here to search

2 Enter a word in the Search box

calculator

3 As you type, relevant apps are displayed. When the one you are seeking appears, click on it to start the app

| All | Apps | Documents | Email | Web | More ▼ |

Best match

Calculator
App

Store

Calculator+ HD >

Calculator X8 >

Search the web

🔍 calculator - See web results >

🔍 calculator

Hot tip

You just have to put in the first couple of letters of an app and Search will automatically suggest results based on this. The more that you type, the more specific the results become. Case does not matter when you are typing a search.

Pin to Start Menu

In most cases, you will want to have quick access to a variety of apps on the Start menu, not just the Windows 10 apps. It is possible to "pin" any app to the Start menu so that it is always readily available. To do this:

 Access the alphabetical list of apps, from the Start button

Hot tip

Apps can be unpinned from the Start menu by right-clicking on them and selecting **Unpin from Start** from the menu that appears.

2 Right-click on an app and click on the **Pin to Start** button

3 The app is pinned to the Start menu, in an unnamed group. It can be repositioned, if required, as with any other app (see page 32)

Pin to Taskbar

All apps can be pinned to the Desktop Taskbar (the bar that appears along the bottom of the Desktop), so that they can be accessed quickly. To do this:

 Click on the **Start** button to access the full list of apps

 Right-click on an app and click on **More** > **Pin to taskbar**

 The app is added to the Taskbar

Hot tip

Apps can be unpinned from the Taskbar by right-clicking on them and selecting **Unpin from taskbar** from the contextual menu that appears.

 Open apps on the Taskbar can also be pinned there by right-clicking on them and selecting **Pin to taskbar**

 Pinned items remain on the Taskbar even once they have been closed

Using the Microsoft Store

The Microsoft Store interface has been updated in the Windows 10 November 2019 Update.

Windows 10 apps can be downloaded from the Microsoft Store.

The third category of apps that can be used with Windows 10 are those that are downloaded from the Microsoft Store. These cover a wide range of topics, and they provide an excellent way to add functionality to Windows 10. To use the Microsoft Store:

1 Click on the **Microsoft Store** tile on the Start menu, or the Taskbar

2 The currently featured apps are displayed on the Home screen

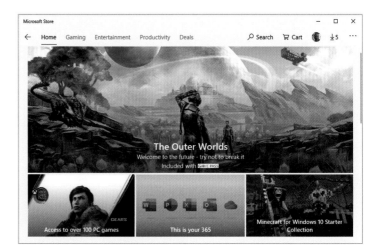

3 Scroll up and down to see additional items and categories

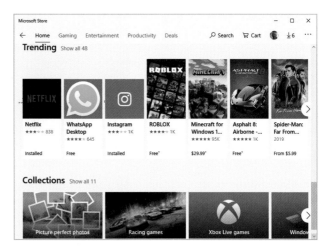

4 Scroll down the Homepage, then click on the **Show all** button next to a category; e.g. **Top free apps**

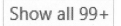

5 The full range of apps for the selected category are displayed. Swipe up and down the page to view them

6 Click on an app to preview it, and for more details

Don't forget

Scroll up and down in Step 6 to view ratings and reviews about the app, and also any additional descriptions.

...cont'd

7 On the **Show all** page, click here to show more headings for looking for apps

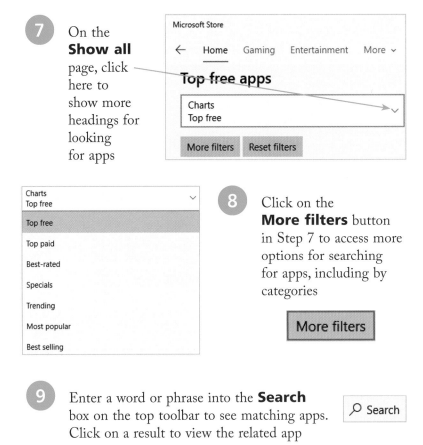

8 Click on the **More filters** button in Step 7 to access more options for searching for apps, including by categories

9 Enter a word or phrase into the **Search** box on the top toolbar to see matching apps. Click on a result to view the related app

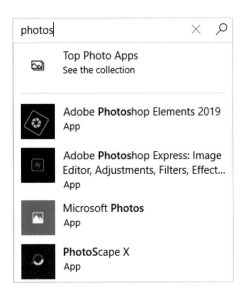

Buying Apps

When you find an app that you want to use, you can download it to your computer. To do this:

1 Access the app and click on the **Get** (or price) button

Don't forget

If there is a fee for an app, this will be displayed instead of the **Get** button. You will need to have credit/debit card details registered on your Microsoft Account in order to buy paid-for apps (**Settings** > **Accounts** > **Your info** > **Manage my Microsoft account**).

2 The app downloads from the Microsoft Store and a **Downloading** message is displayed

Downloading PhotoScape X . 14.31 MB of 219.8 MB

Get more info about faster downloads   4.1 Mb/s

3 The app is added to the Start menu and has a **New** tag next to it. This disappears once the app has been opened

PhotoScape X
New

4 Click on the app to open and use it (initially it will be available under the **Recently added** section of the Start menu, as well as its own alpha listing)

Recently added

PhotoScape X

Don't forget

Once apps have been downloaded they can be reorganized and moved into different groups on the Start menu, or dragged away from their default group to start a new one (see pages 32-33).

Viewing Your Apps

As you download more and more apps from the Microsoft Store you may lose track of which ones you have obtained and when. To help with this, you can review all of the apps you have downloaded, from within the Microsoft Store. To do this:

 Open the Microsoft Store and click on the **Downloads and updates** button

 All of the apps that have been downloaded are displayed

You can reinstall apps from the Downloads section, even if you have previously uninstalled them. If there was a fee for an app, you will not have to pay again to reinstall it.

88

To set apps to be updated automatically, open the Microsoft Store and access Settings from the menu to the right of the Search box. Drag the **Update apps automatically** option **On**.

Microsoft Store							− □ ✕

← Home   Gaming   Entertainment   Productivity   Deals   🔍 Search   🛒 Cart   ♀   ↓1   ···

Downloads

Downloads and updates   Get updates

Available updates (1)   Update all

▪ OneNote   ↓

Recent activity

○ PhotoScape X	App	3.0.3.0		Modified minutes ago
▪ Microsoft Photos	App	2019.19061.17310.0		Modified yesterday
▪ Photos Media Engine...	Add-on	1.0.0.0		Modified yesterday
🐘 Evernote	App	6.20.8626.0		Modified yesterday

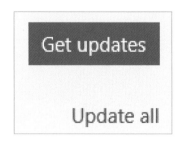 Tap on the **Get updates** button to see if there are any updates for the listed apps

Using Live Tiles

Before any of the Windows 10 apps have been used, they are depicted on the Start menu with tiles of solid color. However, once you open an app it activates the Live Tile feature (if it is supported by that app). This enables the tile to display real-time information from the app, even when it is not the app currently being used. This means that you can view information from your apps, directly from the Start menu. To use Live Tiles:

Don't forget

 Right-click on a tile to select it. If it has Live Tile functionality, click on **More** > **Turn Live Tile on** to activate this feature

The apps with Live Tile functionality include Mail, People, Calendar, Photos, Groove Music, News, Sport and Money. Some of these, such as Mail, require you to first set up an account before Live Tiles can be fully activated.

Live Tiles display real-time text and images from the selected apps. These are updated when there is new information available via the app

Beware

To turn off a Live Tile, right-click on a tile to select it and click on **More** > **Turn Live Tile off**

If you have too many Live Tiles activated at the same time it can become distracting and annoying, with a lot of movement on the Start menu.

Install and Uninstall

Installing apps from a CD or DVD

If the app you want to install is provided on a CD or DVD, you normally just insert the disc. The installation app starts up automatically, and you can follow the instructions to select features and complete the installation. If this does not happen automatically:

 1 Insert the disc and click on this notification window

> **DVD RW Drive (D:) CS5 Design Prem1** ×
> Tap to choose what happens with this disc.

2 Double-click on the **Run Set-up.exe** file link to run it. Follow the on-screen prompts to install the app

> **DVD RW Drive (D:) CS5 Des...**
>
> Choose what to do with this disc.
>
> **Install or run program from your media**
>
> Run Set-up.exe
> Published by Adobe Systems Incorporated
>
> **Other choices**
>
> Import pictures and videos
> Dropbox
>
> Open folder to view files
> File Explorer
>
> Take no action

3 Apps that are installed from a CD or DVD are added to the All apps list on the Start menu

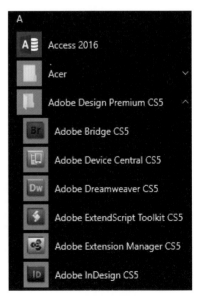

Uninstalling apps

In some previous versions of Windows, apps were uninstalled through the Control Panel. However, in Windows 10, preinstalled Microsoft apps (and Microsoft ones that have been downloaded from the Microsoft Store) can be uninstalled directly from the Start menu. To do this:

 Right-click on an app to access its menu

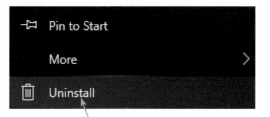

A greater range of apps can be uninstalled in the Windows 10 November 2019 Update. If the **Uninstall** option is not available in Step 1, the app cannot be uninstalled; e.g. the Microsoft Edge app.

2 Click on the **Uninstall** button

3 A window alerts you to the fact that related information will be removed if the app is uninstalled. Click on the **Uninstall** button if you want to continue

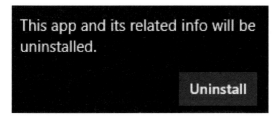

To get to the Control Panel, click on the **Start button**, scroll down to **Windows system**, click on the Down arrow and then select **Control Panel**.

4 If the app is a new Windows 10 one, or has been pinned to the Start menu (or Taskbar), its tile will be removed from its pinned location(s). For other apps, they will no longer be available from the list of apps

Some elements of Windows 10, such as the Control Panel, still refer to apps as programs, but they are the same thing.

If apps have been installed from a CD or DVD they can also still be uninstalled from within the Control Panel. To do this, select the **Programs** section and click on the **Uninstall a Program** link. The installed apps will be displayed. Select one of the apps and click on the **Uninstall/Change** link.

Task Manager

Task Manager lists all the apps and processes running on your computer; you can monitor performance or close an app that is no longer responding.

To open the Task Manager:

As an alternative, press **Ctrl + Alt + Delete** to display the Windows Security screen, from where you can start Task Manager.

1 Right-click on the **Start** button and select **Task Manager**, or press **Ctrl + Shift + Esc**

2 When Task Manager opens, details of the currently running apps are displayed

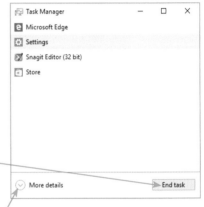

3 If an app is given the status of Not Responding and you cannot wait for Windows to fix things, select the app and click on the **End task** button

If an app stops responding, Windows 10 will try to find the problem and fix it automatically. Using Task Manager to end the app may be quicker, but any unsaved data will be lost.

4 Click on the **More details** button to view detailed information about the running apps. Click on the **Processes** tab to show the system and the current user processes. The total CPU usage and the amount being used by each process are shown as (continually varying) percentages

5 Click on the **Performance** tab to see graphs of recent CPU and memory usage and other details

4 Standard Controls

Even in Windows 10, much of what you do will be with menus, dialog boxes and windows, as used in numerous versions of the operating system. This chapter shows how to use these elements and how you can control and manage working with folders and files in Windows 10.

94 Menus

95 Dialog Boxes

96 Structure of a Window

97 Moving a Window

98 Restoring a Window

99 Resizing a Window

100 Arranging Windows

102 Snap Assist

104 Using Multiple Windows

106 Switching Windows

107 Arranging Icons

108 Closing a Window

Menus

Traditionally, windows have a tabbed Menu bar near the top, displaying the menu options relevant to that particular window. Some Menu bars consist of drop-down menus, and others are in the format of the Ribbon, also known as the Scenic Ribbon.

Drop-down menus

For apps such as Notepad, the Menu bar consists of tabbed drop-down menus:

Beware

The Menu bar is not always displayed in folder windows. Press the **Alt** key to display it temporarily.

1 Open the app and click or tap on one of the Menu bar options to view its details

File		Recent documents
New		1 onedrive1.rtf
Open		2 onedrive1.rtf
Save		
Save as	▶	
Print	▶	

Scenic Ribbon

For apps such as WordPad (and also the File Explorer and Office apps) there is a Ribbon (or Scenic Ribbon) at the top of the window with the Menu bar tabs:

Hot tip

The ellipse (i.e. **...**) indicates that if this option is selected, an associated window with further selections will be displayed.

94

1 Open the app and select one of the Menu bar tabs on the Ribbon to view its details

Document - WordPad

| File | Home | View |

Paste | Cut / Copy | Calibri 11 A A B I U abe x₂ x² A · ✐ · | ≡ ≡ ≡ ≡ ≡ | Picture Paint drawing Date and time Insert object | Find Replace Select all

Clipboard | Font | Paragraph | Insert | Editing

If an option is grayed (dimmed out), it is not available for use at this particular time or is not appropriate.

Some options may have shortcut keys associated with them (e.g. **Alt** + **Up arrow** – Up one level), so you can use these instead of using your mouse. Other examples of shortcut keys are:

Ctrl + **A** – Select All   **Ctrl** + **C** – Copy   **Ctrl** + **V** – Paste
Ctrl + **X** – Cut   **Ctrl** + **Y** – Redo   **Ctrl** + **Z** – Undo

Dialog Boxes

Although simple actions can be made quickly from menu options, more specific settings are made from windows displayed specifically for this purpose. These are called dialog boxes.

Tabs

Some dialog boxes are divided into two or more tabs (grouped options). Only one tab can be viewed at a time.

Checkboxes

Select as many as required. A tick indicates that the option is active. If you select it again it will be turned off. If an option is grayed, it is unavailable and you cannot select it.

Radio buttons

Only one out of a group of radio buttons can be selected. If you select another radio button, the previously selected one is automatically turned off.

Command buttons

OK will save the settings selected and close the dialog box or window. **Cancel** will close, discarding any amended settings. **Apply** will save the settings selected so far but will not close, enabling you to make further changes.

Beware

Dialog boxes are usually fixed-size windows and therefore do not have scroll bars, minimize and maximize buttons or resize pointers.

Hot tip

These examples are from the Folder Options dialog box. To access it, select **Options** on the View section of the Ribbon in File Explorer and select **Change folder and search options**.

Structure of a Window

You can have a window containing icons for further selection, or a window that displays a screen from an app. All these windows are similar in their structure. This example is from the File Explorer (see page 126).

Forward and Back   Address bar   Search box   Title bar area

Quick Access toolbar

Command bar

Navigation pane

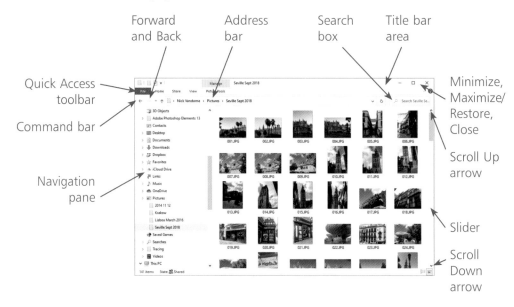

Minimize, Maximize/ Restore, Close

Scroll Up arrow

Slider

Scroll Down arrow

Scroll bars will only appear when there are items that cannot fit into the current size of the window. Here, only a vertical scroll bar is needed.

If you move the mouse pointer over any edge of a window, the pointer changes shape and becomes a double-headed Resize arrow – drag it to change the size of a window (see page 99).

Double-click on an icon to open a window relating to it – in this case a WordPad application window. This window has a Quick access toolbar, Menu bar, Ribbon, ruler, and a Control icon at the top left.

Moving a Window

As long as a window is not maximized – i.e. occupying the whole screen – you can move it. This is especially useful if you have several windows open and need to organize your Desktop.

1 Move the mouse pointer over the Title bar of a window

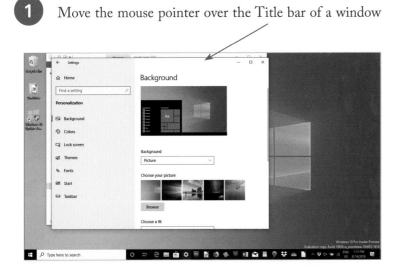

You will see the whole window move, with the full contents displayed and transparency still active while you are dragging the window.

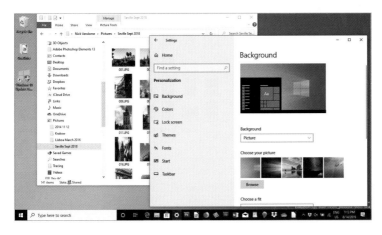

If you have two monitors attached to your system, you can extend your Desktop onto the second monitor and drag a window from one monitor onto the other.

2 Drag the mouse pointer across the Desktop (left-click and hold, or tap and hold as you move)

3 When the window reaches the desired location, release to relocate the window there

If the Title bar has a Control icon, left-click this to show the menu.

Restoring a Window

Within the Desktop environment there are a number of actions that can be performed on the windows within it. A window can be maximized to fill the whole screen, minimized to a button on the Taskbar or restored to the original size.

Hot tip

You can also double-click or tap the **Title bar** to maximize the window. Repeat the process to restore it to the original.

Hot tip

You can also use Snap Assist to maximize, move or resize windows (see pages 102-103).

Original size window   Maximize button   Maximized window

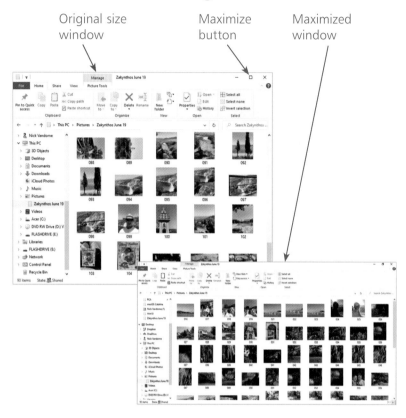

Don't forget

You can right-click the Title bar area to display the Control context menu.

Whether a window is maximized or original size, click on the **Minimize** button (left of the top-right three buttons) to reduce the window to its Taskbar icon. This will create space on the Desktop for you to work in other windows. When you want to restore the reduced window, simply select its **Taskbar** icon.

The middle button is the Maximize button. Or, if the window is already maximized, the button changes to the Restore button.

Click **Close**, the third button, when you want to close an app or to close a window.

98

Resizing a Window

If a window is not maximized or minimized, it can be resized.

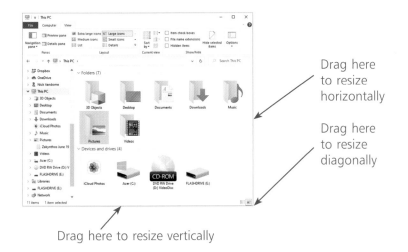

Drag here to resize horizontally

Drag here to resize diagonally

Drag here to resize vertically

Hot tip

Resize and move all of the windows on your Desktop to organize the layout to the way you prefer to work, or see pages 100-101 for other ways of arranging windows.

1 Place the mouse arrow anywhere on the edge of a window or on any of the corners. The pointer will change to a double-headed Resize arrow

Beware

The Size command is not available if the window is maximized.

2 Click, or tap, and drag the arrow outwards to increase the size of the window, or inwards to reduce the size

Resizing a window using keyboard shortcuts

Alternatively, you may want to use the keyboard keys to resize a window.

1 Press **Alt** + **Space bar**

2 Press **S** and the mouse pointer will change to a four-headed arrow

3 Use the Left, Right, Up or Down arrow keys on your keyboard to adjust the size of the window

4 Press **Enter** when the window is resized as required

Arranging Windows

If you have several windows open on your Desktop and you want to automatically rearrange them neatly, rather than resize and move each one individually, use the Cascade or Tile options.

Only open windows are arranged, not minimized windows. Also, fixed-size windows will get a proportional share of the screen, but they will not be resized.

1 Right-click a clear area on the Taskbar to display a context menu and select one of the arrangement options

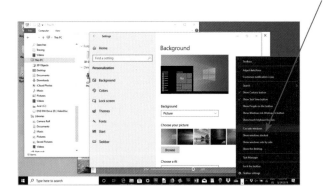

100

2 **Cascade windows** overlaps all open windows, revealing the Title bar areas and resizing the windows equally

Don't forget

When you right-click the Taskbar, all windows are deselected, so you must click or tap a window to select it and make it currently active.

3 **Show windows stacked** resizes windows equally and displays them across the screen in rows

Hot tip

When you have used a function to arrange windows, a matching Undo function is added to the Taskbar context menu.

4 **Show windows side by side** resizes windows equally and displays them across the screen in columns

...cont'd

When you have a number of windows open on the Desktop, you might wish to see what is hidden underneath. For this, Windows 10 offers the Peek function.

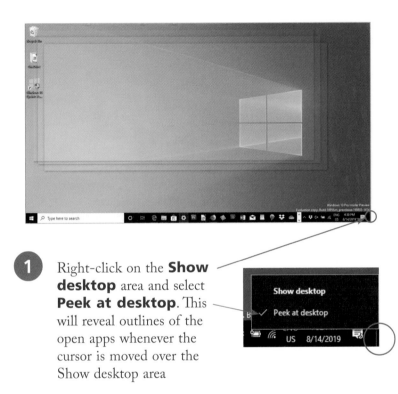

1 Right-click on the **Show desktop** area and select **Peek at desktop**. This will reveal outlines of the open apps whenever the cursor is moved over the Show desktop area

2 Select the **Show desktop** option in Step 1 to show just the Desktop when the cursor is moved over the Show desktop area

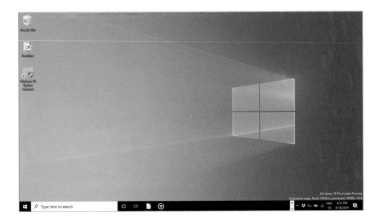

Hot tip

The **Show desktop** button is on the far right of the Taskbar, next to the Notification area button.

Snap Assist

Snap Assist provides a set of methods for resizing and moving windows around the Desktop.

Maximize fully

If the window you want to maximize is not the current one, click on it first before carrying out the maximize operation.

Click (or tap) and hold the Title bar and drag the window up the screen. As the mouse pointer reaches the top edge of the screen, the window maximizes. The shortcut is **WinKey** + **Up arrow**.

Maximize vertically

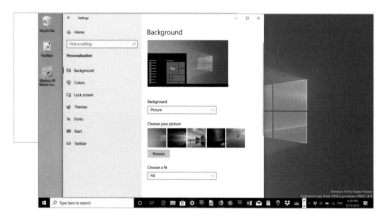

Alternatively, you can drag the bottom border of the window towards the bottom edge of the screen to maximize it vertically.

Click or tap and hold the top border of the window (until it turns into a double-headed arrow), and drag it towards the top edge of the screen. When the mouse pointer reaches the edge of the screen, the window will maximize in the vertical direction only. The shortcut is **WinKey** + **Shift** + **Up arrow**.

Snap to the left

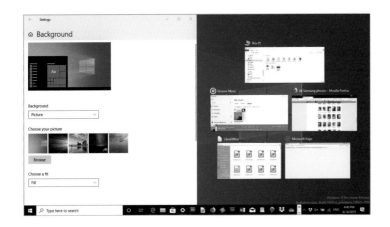

When you click the Title bar on an app such as WordPad, be sure to avoid the tools on the Quick access toolbar.

To position the window to fill the left-hand side of the screen, click (or tap) the Title bar and drag it to the left. As the mouse pointer reaches the left edge, the window resizes to fill half of the screen. The shortcut is **WinKey** + **Left arrow**. If other apps are open they will be shown as thumbnails in the right-hand panel.

Snap to the right

To position the window to fill the right-hand side of the screen, click or tap the Title bar and drag it to the right. As the mouse pointer reaches the right edge, the window resizes to fill half of the screen. The shortcut key is **WinKey** + **Right arrow**.

Compare two windows

Snap one of the windows to the left and the other window to the right.

Restore

Drag the Title bar of a maximized or snapped window away from the edge of the screen and the window will return to its previous size (though not the same position). The shortcut is **WinKey** + **Down arrow**.

Alternatively, to make the two windows the only open (not minimized) windows, right-click the Taskbar, and then choose the option to **Show windows side by side**.

Double-clicking or tapping the Title bar will also reverse the maximize or snap. This restores size and position.

Using Multiple Windows

Windows 10 provides great flexibility when it comes to working with windows: it is possible to display up to four active windows at a time, rather than just two side by side: To do this:

 Open an app and drag its window to the left-hand side of the screen, until it snaps left and takes up the left half of the screen

Don't forget

Apps can be arranged in multiple windows in any order; e.g. one can be placed in the right-hand corner and then one on the left-hand side.

 Open a second app and drag its window to the right-hand side of the screen, until it snaps right and takes up the right half of the screen

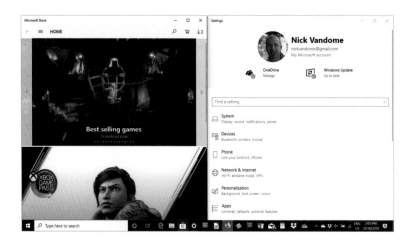

3 Open a third app and drag its window into the top left-hand corner of the screen. The left-hand side of the screen will display the two apps

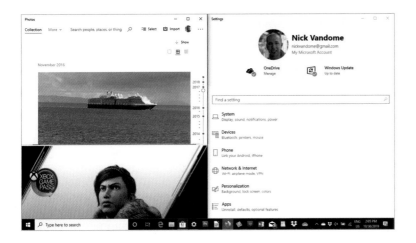

4 Open a fourth app and drag its window into the top right-hand corner of the screen. The right-hand side of the screen will display the two apps

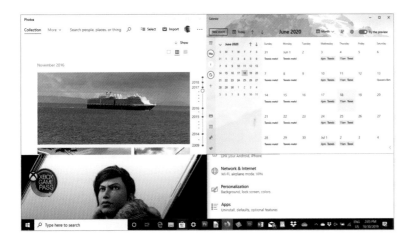

Apps can be "unsnapped" from their positions, by clicking and holding on the Title bar and dragging them into a new position.

Switching Windows

If you have several windows open on your Desktop, only one will be active. This will be the foremost window and it has its Title bar, Menu bar and outside window frame highlighted. If you have more than one window displayed on the Desktop, select anywhere inside a window that is not active to activate it and switch to it.

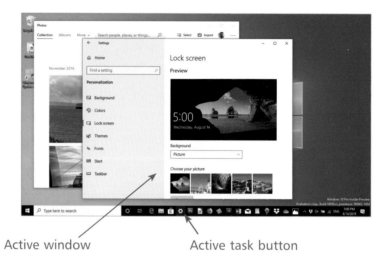

Active window   Active task button

Another method of switching windows is to use the Taskbar at the bottom. Every window that is open has an icon button created automatically on the Taskbar. Therefore, it does not matter if the window you want to switch to is overlaid with others and you cannot see it. Just select the button for it in the Taskbar and the window will be moved to the front and made active.

Move the mouse pointer over a task button, and a Live Preview is displayed (one for each window if there are multiple tasks).

You can click on the preview to select that item and bring its window to the front of the Desktop.

Arranging Icons

You can rearrange the order of the items in your folders or on your Desktop in many different ways.

 Right-click in a clear area (of the Desktop or folder window) to display a shortcut context menu

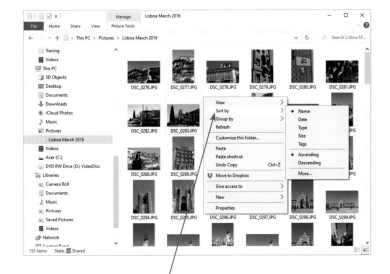

2 Move the pointer over **Sort by** to reveal the submenu of sorting options and click or tap the **Name** option, for example, to sort all the file icons in ascending name order

Hot tip

Select the **View** button in Step 1 to cycle through a range of views. Click or tap the **Down arrow** to see the full set of options.

3 Select **Name** a second time and the files will be sorted in descending name order

Group by

You can select **Group by** for folder windows (but not for the Desktop). This groups your files and folders alphabetically by name, size, type, etc.

Closing a Window

When you have finished with a window you will need to close it. There are several ways of doing this – use the method that is easiest and the most appropriate at the time.

Open window
If the top-right corner of the window is visible on the Desktop:

 Select the **Close** button on the Title bar

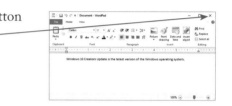

Save your work before closing any app window in which you have been working. However, Windows will prompt you if you forget.

Minimized window
For a window that is minimized or one that is hidden behind other windows:

 Move the mouse pointer over the associated Taskbar icon button

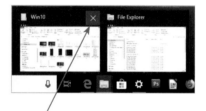

 Select the **Close** button on the Live Preview for the task

Control menu
If only part of the window is visible on the Desktop:

1 Select the **Control** icon (top-left corner) or right-click the Title bar

2 Select **Close** on the Control menu

Keyboard
To close any type of window, use this key combination:

 Select the window to make it the current, active window, then press **Alt** + **F4** to close the window

5 Customizing Windows

The Desktop environment is still an important one in Windows 10, and this chapter looks at how to work with it and personalize the elements of Windows 10 to your own requirements and preferences, with colors, themes and sounds.

110 Personalization

112 Using Themes

114 Changing Color Themes

116 Lock Screen Settings

118 Changing Sound

119 Desktop Icons

120 Screen Resolution

121 Managing Storage

122 Ease of Access

124 Date and Time Functions

Personalization

Customizing the look and feel of Windows 10 is a good way to make it feel like it is your own personal device. This can be done with some of the options in the Personalization section of the Settings app. To do this:

Open the **Settings** app and click on the **Personalization** button

> Personalization
> Background, lock screen, colors

Click on the **Background** button to select a Desktop background. Select **Picture** in the Background box and click to select a picture or click on the **Browse** button to select one of your own pictures

Click in the **Choose a fit** box in Step 2 to specify how the picture fills the background screen. The options are: Fill, Fit, Stretch, Tile, Center, and Span.

Click on the **Colors** button to select an accent color for the current background, Start menu and Taskbar. It can also be used to create color themes – see pages 114-115

4 Check this box **Off** to disable the automatic selection for the accent color

Choose your accent color

☐ Automatically pick an accent color from my background

Recent colors

Windows colors

5 Click on one of the colors to select it for the accent color

6 Drag this button **On** to make the Start menu, Taskbar and Action Center transparent

Transparency effects

⬤ On

7 Click on these buttons to use the color selected in Step 5 on the Start menu, Taskbar, Action Center, and Title bars

Show accent color on the following surfaces

☑ Start, taskbar, and action center

☑ Title bars and window borders

8 Click on the **Custom color** button underneath the color palette

+ Custom color

9 Click on the color graph to select a customized accent color. Drag the slider underneath the graph to amend the selected color

Choose a custom accent color

Blue

More ⌄

Color preview

10 Click on the **Done** button to use the color selected in Step 9

Preview

Done   Cancel

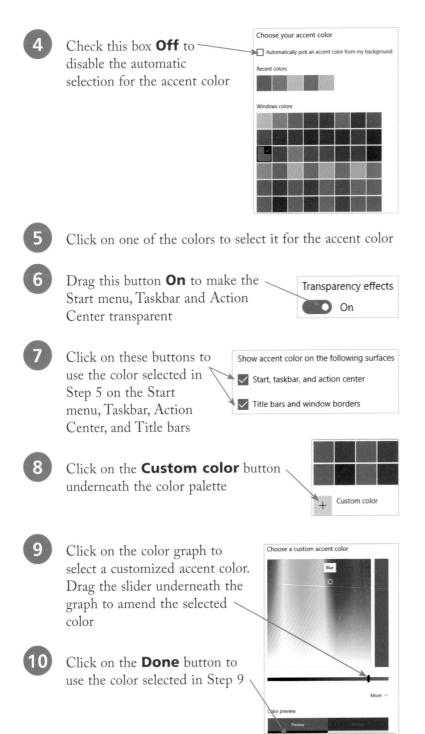

Using Themes

Themes in the Windows 10 can be used to customize several items for the look and feel of Windows:

1 Open **Settings** and click on the **Personalization** button

2 Click on the **Themes** button

3 The current theme is displayed

4 Make a selection for a customized theme, using **Background**, **Color**, **Sounds** and **Mouse cursor**

5 The selections for the customized theme are shown in the **Current theme** preview window

6 Click on the **Save theme** button to use it for the current theme

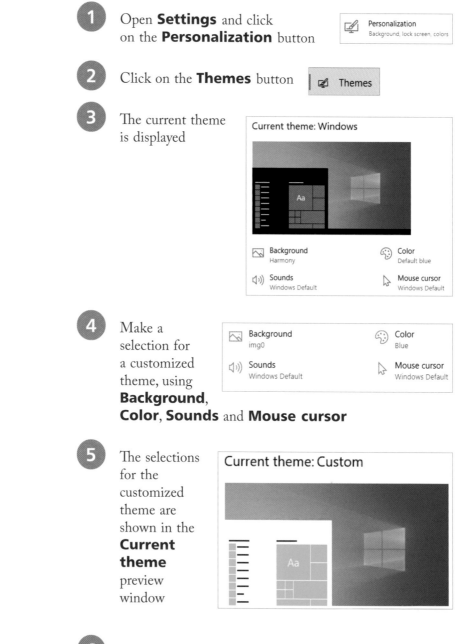

7 Click on one of the preset themes to select it rather than customizing one

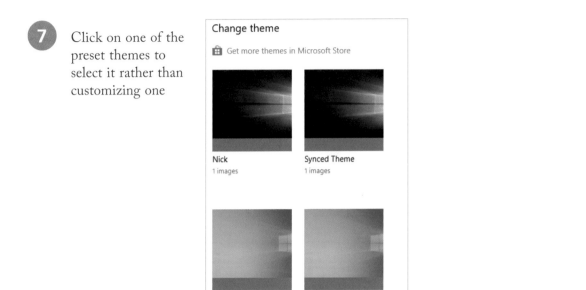

Change theme

🏬 Get more themes in Microsoft Store

Nick
1 images

Synced Theme
1 images

Windows
1 images

Windows (light)
1 images

8 All of the elements of the preset theme are displayed in the preview window

Current theme: Windows 10

Aa

🖼 Background
Slideshow (5 images)

🎨 Color
Automatic

🔊 Sounds
Windows Default

☐ Mouse cursor
Windows Default

9 Click on **Get more themes in Microsoft Store** to download more themes that can be used on your PC

🏬 Get more themes in Microsoft Store

Changing Color Themes

The Colors option in the Personalization section of the Settings app can be used to edit the overall color scheme of Windows 10, including a new Light Theme that applies a crisper look and feel to all elements of the Windows 10 interface. To create this:

The Color Theme options is a new feature in the Windows 10 November 2019 Update.

1 Open the **Settings** app and click on the **Personalization** button

Personalization
Background, lock screen, colors

2 Click on the **Colors** button

Colors

3 Click in the **Choose your color** box

Choose your color
Custom ⌄

4 Click on the **Light** option to apply a Light Theme for the elements of Windows 10

Choose your color
Light
Dark
Custom

The Color Themes do not alter the Desktop background. This is done in **Settings** > **Personalization** > **Background**.

5 The Light Theme is also applied to the Start menu and the Taskbar

114

6 If the **Dark** option is selected in Step 4, the background and foreground will be inverted

Settings

Home

Find a setting

Personalization

Background

Colors

Lock screen

Themes

Fonts

Start

Taskbar

Colors

Sample Text

Aa

Choose your color

Dark

Transparency effects

On

Choose your accent color

☐ Automatically pick an accent color from my background

Recent colors

Hot tip

The Dark Theme for apps can be useful in the evening, or low-level lighting, as it can be more relaxing on the eyes when looking at content on the screen.

7 Click on the **Custom** button in Step 4 to select specific settings for the Windows interface and the appearance of apps. For instance, the Windows mode could be Dark, and the default app mode could be Light

Choose your color

Custom

Choose your default Windows mode

○ Light

◉ Dark

Choose your default app mode

◉ Light

○ Dark

115

Lock Screen Settings

The Settings app enables you to set the appearance of the Lock screen and the Start menu, and to select an account photo. To do this, first access the Settings:

1 Open the **Settings** app and click on the **Personalization** button

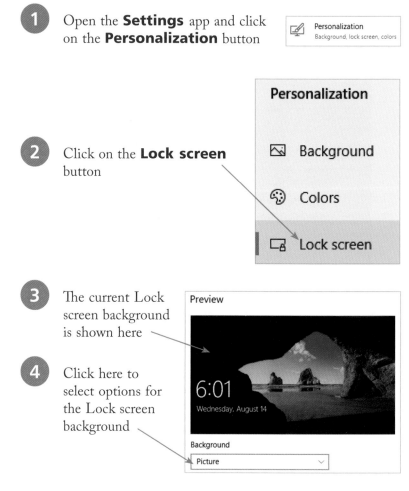

2 Click on the **Lock screen** button

3 The current Lock screen background is shown here

4 Click here to select options for the Lock screen background

If **Slideshow** is selected in Step 5, you will then have the option to choose an album of photos to use as the slideshow for the Lock screen background.

5 Select one of the Lock screen background options from **Windows spotlight**, **Picture** or **Slideshow**

6 For the Picture option, click on the **Browse** button to select your own picture

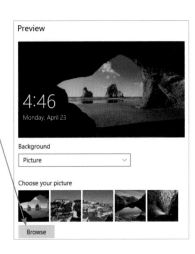

7 Select an image and click on **Choose picture** to add this to the background options for the Lock screen

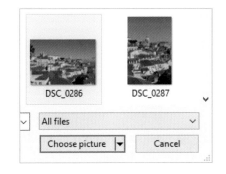

If you use your own images for the Lock screen background, these will remain available on the thumbnail row even if you switch to another image for the background.

8 Other options for the Lock screen include selecting apps that display their detailed or quick status, options for screen timeout when not in use, and screen saver settings

Choose an app to show detailed status

Choose apps to show quick status

Show lock screen background picture on the sign-in screen

On

Cortana lock screen settings

Screen timeout settings

Screen saver settings

117

Changing Sound

 Select **Settings** >
Personalization > **Themes**

 Click on the **Sounds** button
and click on the Sounds tab in
the Sound window

Don't forget

Click the Down arrow on
the Sound Scheme drop-
down bar to try out a
different scheme.

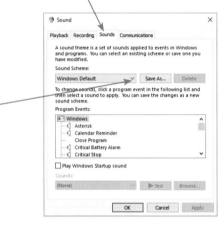

118

Hot tip

If you do not want to
have sounds associated
with Windows events,
select **No Sounds** from
the options in the drop-
down list in Step 1.

 Select a Program Event and click the **Test** button to hear
the associated sound

 Browse to locate a new sound file (file type .wav), then
select **Test** to preview the effect

5 Make any other changes, then select **Save As...**, and
provide a name for your modified sound scheme

Desktop Icons

To control the display of icons on the Desktop:

1 Right-click on the Desktop, click **View** and select **Show desktop icons**. A check mark is added

2 To resize the icons, display the View menu as above and click **Large icons**, **Medium icons** or **Small icons**

3 To remove the check mark and hide all the icons, display the View menu and select **Show desktop icons** again

4 To choose which of the system icons appear, open **Settings** and select **Personalization > Themes > Desktop icon settings** (under **Related Settings**)

5 Select or clear the boxes to show or hide icons as required, then click **Apply** and **OK** to confirm the changes

You can use the scroll wheel on your mouse to resize desktop icons. On the Desktop, hold down **Ctrl** as you roll the wheel up or down.

When you right-click the Desktop, you will find customization functions **Display settings** and **Personalize** on the context menu displayed.

The **Control Panel** is one of the options in Step 5 and a link to it can be added to the Desktop in this way.

Screen Resolution

If you have a high-resolution screen, you may find that the text, as well as the icons, is too small. You can increase the effective size by reducing the screen resolution.

If you want to use the Snap Assist function as shown on pages 102-103 you need to have a minimum screen resolution of 1366 x 768.

If you have an LCD monitor or a laptop computer, you are recommended to stay with the native resolution, normally the highest.

120

1 Open the **Settings** app, select **System** and then click on the **Display** button

🖵 Display

2 Drag this slider to change the overall brightness of items on your screen (if this option is not showing, it may be that you can only change the brightness of the screen on the monitor itself)

Display

Brightness and color

Change brightness for the built-in display

Night light (off until 8:55 PM)
On

Night light settings

3 Click the drop-down arrow next to **Display orientation** to switch the view to **Portrait**; e.g. for tablet PCs

Display resolution

1366 × 768 (Recommended)

Display orientation

Landscape

4 Click here to change the screen resolution. Select a new resolution value from the list

Display resolution

1366 × 768 (Recommended)

1360 × 768

1280 × 768

1280 × 720

1280 × 600

1024 × 768

800 × 600

5 Click on the **Keep changes** button to change the screen resolution

Keep changes Revert

Managing Storage

Computer storage is sometimes a feature that is taken for granted and left untouched. However, with Windows 10 there are some options for customizing how storage functions on your computer. To use these:

Open the **Settings** app, select **System** and then click on the **Storage** button

At the top of the window, the current storage is displayed, with the amount used shown by a colored bar

> Acer (C:) - 698 GB
> 223 GB used　　　　　　　　　　　　　475 GB free

Drag the **Storage** button **On** to enable Windows to free up storage space by deleting redundant files and items in the Recycle Bin

> ## Storage
>
> Storage Sense can automatically free up space by getting rid of files you don't need, like temporary files and content in your recycle bin.
>
> ◯ On

The amount of storage space taken up by different types of content is displayed. Click on an item to view more details about it and manage its amount of storage space

> This is how your storage is used and how you can free up space.
>
> 🗁　Documents　　　　　　　　　　　66.5 GB
> 　　Manage the Documents folder
>
> 🗑　Temporary files　　　　　　　　　50.5 GB
> 　　Choose which temporary files to remove
>
> 🖥　Apps & features　　　　　　　　　33.0 GB
> 　　Uninstall unused or undesired apps & features
>
> 🖼　Pictures　　　　　　　　　　　　20.7 GB
> 　　Manage the Pictures folder
>
> 📄　Other　　　　　　　　　　　　　3.62 GB
> 　　Manage other large folders
>
> Show more categories

Don't forget

Under the **More storage settings** heading, click on **Change where new content is saved**.

> More storage settings
>
> View storage usage on other drives
>
> Change where new content is saved

Ease of Access

Making Windows 10 accessible for as wide a range of users as possible is an important consideration, and there are a range of accessibility settings that can be used for this. To do this:

1 Open **Settings** and click on the **Ease of Access** button

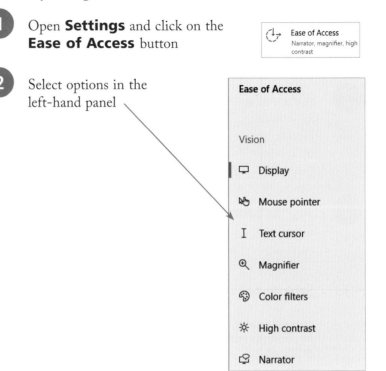

Ease of Access
Narrator, magnifier, high contrast

2 Select options in the left-hand panel

Ease of Access

Vision

- 🖵 Display
- 🖑 Mouse pointer
- I Text cursor
- 🔍 Magnifier
- 🎨 Color filters
- ☼ High contrast
- 🗪 Narrator

Don't forget

The settings for the Narrator can be used to specify the items on the screen that are read out. For some items, such as buttons and controls, there is an audio description of the item.

3 Each option has settings that can be applied. For instance, drag the **Narrator** button from **Off** to **On** to enable items to be read out on the screen

Don't forget

There is also a Braille option that can be accessed towards the bottom of the Narrator window. This has to be used in conjunction with third-party software that communicates with a Braille display.

Narrator

Narrator is a screen reader that describes what's on your screen so you can use that information to navigate your device. It can be controlled by keyboard, touch, and mouse.

Use Narrator

Turn on Narrator

 Off

Open Narrator Home

View the complete guide to Narrator online

4 Select **Magnifier** in Step 1, and turn Magnifier **On** to activate the magnifying glass. Move this over areas of the screen to magnify them

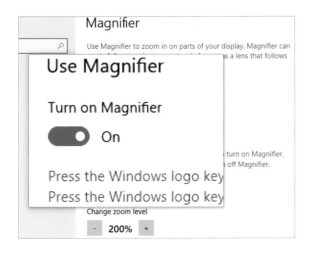

Hot tip

In the **Magnifier** option, click the **Invert colors** checkbox **On**, to highlight the area underneath the magnifier in inverted colors to the rest of the screen, to make it stand out more.

> ☑ Invert colors
> Press Ctrl + Alt + I to invert colors.

5 Select the **High contrast** option in Step 2 and drag the **Turn on high contrast** button **On**, then click in the **Choose a theme** box to select a color theme for text and background for users who find it difficult reading black text on a white background

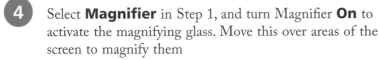

123

Date and Time Functions

To change the format Windows uses to display dates and times:

 Select the **Settings >
Time & Language** option

Time & Language
Speech, region, date

 Click on the **Date & time**
button

🕤 Date & time

Don't forget

If the **Set time automatically** button is **Off**, click on the **Change** button below **Set the date and time manually** to set a manual date and time.

Set the date and time manually
Change

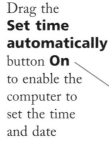 Drag the
**Set time
automatically**
button **On**
to enable the
computer to
set the time
and date

Date & time

Current date and time

12:36 PM, Thursday, August 15, 2019

Set time automatically
⬤ On

Set time zone automatically
⬤ Off

Set the date and time manually
Change

Synchronize your clock
Last successful time synchronization: 8/14/2019 1:22:47 PM
Time server: time.windows.com
Sync now

④ Click on the
Region
button to set
the default
geographical
region for the
computer

🌐 Region

Region

Country or region

United States ⌄

Windows and apps might use your country or region to give you local content.

Regional format

Current format: English (United States)

Recommended [English (United States)] ⌄

Windows formats dates and times based on your language and regional preferences.

⑤ Click on the **Language** button to set
the default language for the computer

A字 Language

6 File Explorer

The File Explorer is at the heart of working with the files on your computer, and you can use it to browse all of the information on your computer and on the local network. This chapter shows how you can use the Scenic Ribbon function, modify the views in File Explorer, use the Quick access folder, sort the contents, and customize the style and appearance.

126 Opening File Explorer

127 The Taskbar

128 Libraries

129 Scenic Ribbon

131 This PC Folder

132 Quick Access

134 Exploring Drives

136 Address Bar

138 Navigation Panes

140 Changing Views

141 Sorting

142 Filtering

143 Grouping

144 Folder Options

Opening File Explorer

Although File Explorer (formerly called Windows Explorer) is not necessarily one of the first apps that you will use with Windows 10, it still plays an important role in organizing your folders and files. To access File Explorer:

 1 From the Desktop, click on this icon on the Taskbar, or

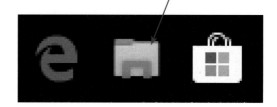

2 Press **WinKey** + **E**, and File Explorer opens at the **Quick access** folder

3 When File Explorer is opened, click on the **This PC** option to view the top-level items on your computer, including the main folders, your hard drive and any removable devices that are connected

This PC displays files from different locations as a single collection, without actually moving any files.

You can click on the **Start** button and access File Explorer from here too.

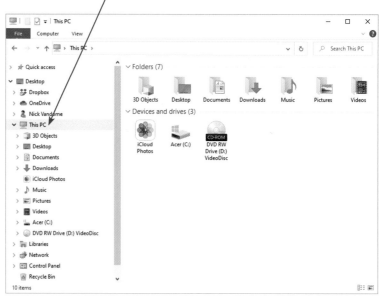

The Taskbar

The Taskbar is visible at the bottom of the screen and displays
thumbnails of the apps that have been added there. To illustrate
the range of functions that it supports:

 Open items are displayed
on the Taskbar at the
bottom of the window

(denoted by a white or colored line underneath the
item's icon – the color depends on your choices in the
Personalization settings)

 Right-click an open item on the
Taskbar to view open files within
the items and also recently viewed
pages within it

Hot tip

File Explorer (also known
as Explorer) is the
program Explorer.exe. It
handles the file system
and user interfaces, and
is sometimes referred to
as the Windows Shell.

127

Pinned

Downloads
Desktop
Pictures
iCloud Photos
F:\
Recent folders
Dropbox
Downloads
Downloads
FCA

Frequent

Win10
Lisboa March 2016
Nick Vandome (1)

File Explorer
Unpin from taskbar
Close window

Move the mouse pointer over the
File Explorer icon to see previews
of the open folder windows that
File Explorer is managing (if File
Explorer is open)

Libraries

File Explorer can use the Library for accessing the files and folders on your computer and network. Each Library displays files from several locations. Initially, there are five Libraries defined:

● **Camera Roll**, which is the default folder for photos captured on your computer (if it has a camera attached).

● **Documents**, which is the default folder for files such as those created with word processing or presentation apps.

● **Music**, which is the default folder for music bought from the online Microsoft Store, or added yourself.

● **Pictures**, which is the default folder for your photos.

● **Videos**, which is the default folder for your videos.

To view the Pictures Library, for example:

 Select **Libraries > Pictures** in the Navigation pane

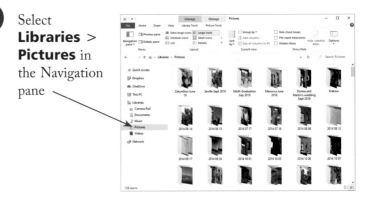

To add another folder to the Pictures library:

 Right-click in the Pictures Library window and select **New > Folder**

2 Click on the folder name and overwrite it with a new title

Beware

In Windows 10 the Libraries are not visible by default. To show them, click on the View button on the Scenic Ribbon, click on the **Navigation pane** button and click on the **Show libraries** button so that a tick appears.

Hot tip

You can also right-click the folder name in the Navigation pane folder list, to display the **New > Folder** menu.

Scenic Ribbon

The navigation and functionality in the Libraries is provided by the Scenic Ribbon at the top of the window. This has options for the Library itself and also the type of content that is being viewed.

 Click on the tabs at the top of the Library window to view associated tools

Don't forget

The Scenic Ribbon is also referred to as just the Ribbon.

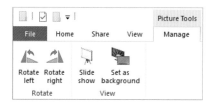 Click on the Library Tools tab to view the menus for the whole Library (see below)

 Click on the content tab (Picture Tools in this example) to view menus for the selected content

Library File menu
This contains options for opening a new window, closing the current window or moving to a frequently visited location in the Library.

Don't forget

The **File** button in the Ribbon remains highlighted in blue, regardless of which other menu is accessed.

Library Home menu
This contains options for copying and pasting, moving, deleting and renaming selected items. You can also create new folders, view folder properties and select all items in a folder.

...cont'd

Library Share menu

This contains options for sharing selected items, by sending them to another user on the computer, burning them to a CD or DVD, creating a compressed Zip file or sending the items to a printer.

Library View menu

This contains options for how you view the items in the current active folder (see page 140).

Hot tip

Click on the **Options** button on the View menu to set additional options for the operation of a folder and how items are displayed within it.

Library Manage menu

This contains options for managing specific Libraries. Click on the **Manage library** button to add additional folders to the one currently being viewed.

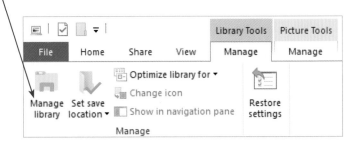

Library menu options

If there is a down-pointing arrow next to an item on a Library menu, click it to see additional options, such as the **Optimize library for** button, which optimizes the folder for specific types of content.

This PC Folder

One of the best ways to look at the contents of your computer involves using the This PC folder. To open this:

1 Open File Explorer and select **This PC** in the Navigation pane

Navigation pane   Location   Search box

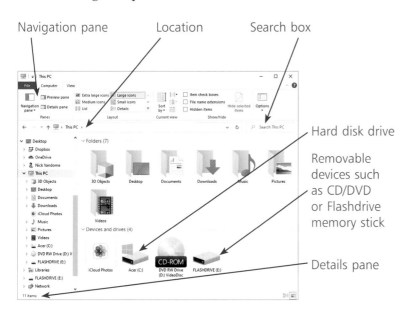

Hard disk drive

Removable devices such as CD/DVD or Flashdrive memory stick

Details pane

Don't forget

The Navigation pane provides the facilities you require to move between folders and drives.

2 Select items and double-click to view their contents

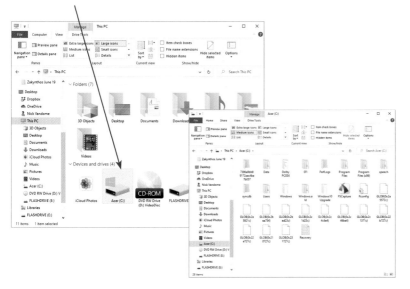

Quick Access

When working with files and folders there will probably be items that you access on a regular basis. The Quick access section of the File Explorer can be used to view the items that you have most recently accessed, and also to pin your most frequently used and favorite items. To use the Quick access section:

1 Click on the right-pointing arrow on the **Quick access** button in the File Explorer Navigation pane so that it becomes downwards-pointing

132

2 In the main window, your frequently used folders and most recently used files are displayed

3 The folders are also listed underneath the **Quick access** button in the Navigation pane

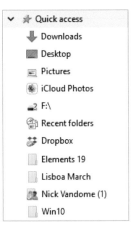

Adding items to Quick access

The folders that you access and use most frequently can be pinned to the Quick access section. This does not physically move them; it just creates a shortcut within Quick access. To do this:

1 Right-click on the folder you want to pin, and click on **Pin to Quick access**

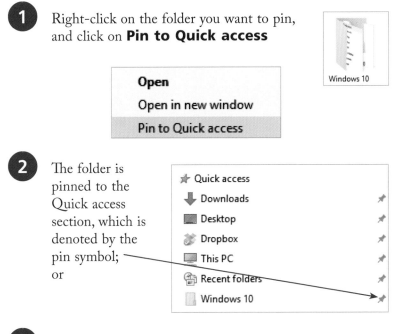

2 The folder is pinned to the Quick access section, which is denoted by the pin symbol; or

3 Drag the folder over the Quick access button until the **Pin to Quick access** option appears, and release

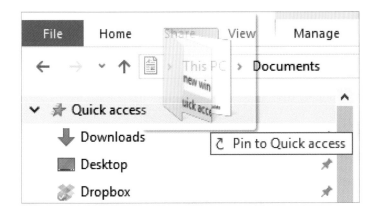

To unpin an item from Quick access, right-click on it and click on **Unpin from Quick access**.

Exploring Drives

Explore the contents of any drive from the This PC folder:

 Select one of the drive icons – for example, the **Flashdrive** removable storage device

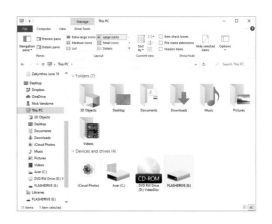

 Double-click the **Flashdrive** device icon (or select it and press **Enter**) to display the files and folders that it contains

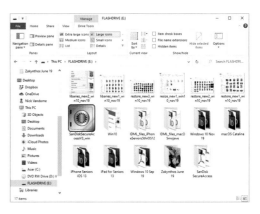

 Double-click a folder entry (e.g. Win10) and select one of the files that it contains

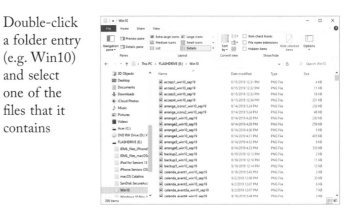

Double-click the file icon and press **Enter** to open the file using the associated application

Don't forget

Press the **Back arrow** to go to the previous library or location, or click the **Down arrow** to select from the list of viewed locations. Click the **Up arrow** to move up one level.

134

You can see all the folder entries in This PC in a structured list:

 Double-click the **This PC** entry in the Navigation pane

 The computer's folders are displayed, and the fixed drives plus any removable drives with media inserted are listed

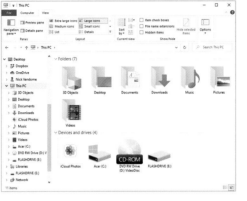

You can also explore the folders in Quick access, Libraries and Network of attached computers.

 Select the ❯ right-pointing arrow next to a heading level, to expand that entry to the next level

Resize the Navigation pane horizontally using the Stretch arrow, and traverse folder lists using the vertical scroll bar.

 Select the ❮ down-pointing arrow to collapse the entries to that heading level

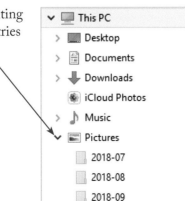

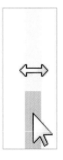

135

Address Bar

The Address bar at the top of File Explorer displays the current location as a set of names separated by arrows, and offers another way to navigate between libraries and locations.

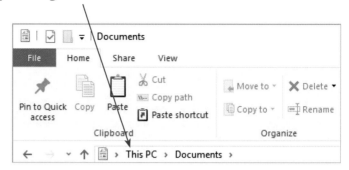

1 To go to a location that is named in the address, click on that name in the Address bar; e.g. Documents

2 To select a subfolder of a library or location named in the Address bar, click on the arrow to the right

3 Click one of the entries to open it in place of the current location

When you are viewing a drive rather than a library, the Address bar shows the drive and its folders, and allows you to navigate amongst these.

...cont'd

You can specify a new location using the Address bar:

 Click on the Address bar in the blank space to the right of the set of names, and the full path is displayed

← → ˅ ↑ 📄 > This PC > Documents >

 Type the complete folder path, e.g. C:\Users\Public (or click in the path and amend the values), then press **Enter**

← → ˅ ↑ 📄 C:\Users\Public|

Hot tip

The path is highlighted, so typing a new path will completely replace the original values.

 The specified location will be displayed

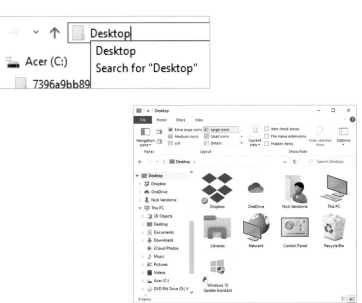

If you want a common location such as Desktop, just type the name alone and press **Enter**, and the location will be displayed:

Hot tip

You can switch to exploring the internet, by typing a web page address. The Microsoft Edge browser will be launched in a separate window.

Navigation Panes

The normal view for File Explorer includes the Navigation pane. There is also a Preview pane and a Details pane available.

You can choose different panes to display:

1 Open File Explorer and click on the **View** tab. This will open the Ribbon

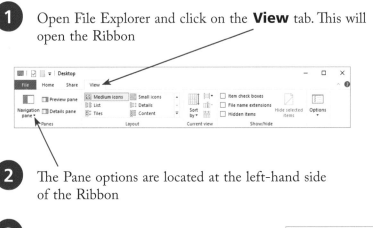

2 The Pane options are located at the left-hand side of the Ribbon

3 Click on the **Navigation pane** button to view this format. This appears down the left-hand side

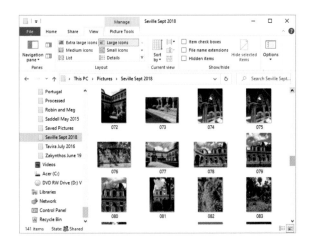

Beware

If you check **Off** the Navigation pane in Step 4, the left-hand panel will not be visible in File Explorer.

4 Click on the arrow on the **Navigation pane** button and click here to show or hide the Navigation pane. There are also options here for showing or hiding the libraries

5 Click on the **Preview pane** button to view a preview of the folder or file selected in the main window

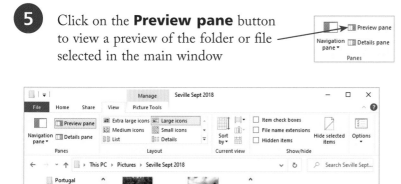

The Preview pane is particularly useful if you are working in the Pictures library.

6 Click on the **Details pane** button to view additional information about the folder or file selected in the main window

Changing Views

You can change the size and appearance of the file and folder icons in your folders, using the View tab on the Ribbon.

 Open the folder you would like to change and click on the **View** tab on the Ribbon. Select one of the options for viewing content in the folder

The way items are displayed within folders can also be set within Folder Options (see page 144).

 Click on different items to change the appearance of icons, such as from the Layout section

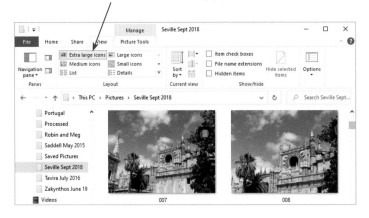 Hover the cursor over each **View** setting to preview. Click the mouse button to apply that view

Sorting

Windows 10 allows you to sort your files in the drive or folder by various attributes or descriptors.

 Open the folder, click on **View > Details** and select the attribute header that you want to sort by; e.g. Date

2 The entries are sorted into ascending order by the selected attribute. The header is shaded and a sort symbol ⌃ added

Right-click on a column heading in Steps 2 and 3 to select which column headings appear; e.g. Date, Size, Type, etc.

This PC > Pictures > Seville Sept 2018		
Portugal ⌃	Name ⌃	Date
Processed	001	9/3/2018 8:33 PM
Robin and Meg	002	9/3/2018 8:33 PM
Saddell May 2015	003	9/3/2018 8:36 PM
Saved Pictures	004	9/3/2018 8:36 PM
Seville Sept 2018	005	9/3/2018 8:45 PM
Tavira July 2016	006	9/3/2018 8:47 PM

3 Select the header again. The order is reversed and the header now shows an inverted sort symbol ⌄

Note that any subfolders within your folder will be sorted to the end of the list when you reverse the sequence. Libraries are an exception, and keep folders at the top (in the appropriate sort order).

This PC > Pictures > Seville Sept 2018		
Portugal ⌃	Name ⌄	Date
Processed	140	9/6/2018 2:51 PM
Robin and Meg	139	9/6/2018 2:46 PM
Saddell May 2015	138	9/6/2018 2:14 PM
Saved Pictures	137	9/6/2018 1:54 PM
Seville Sept 2018	136	9/6/2018 1:54 PM
Tavira July 2016	135	9/6/2018 1:41 PM

4 The contents will remain sorted in the selected sequence, even if you switch to a different folder view

Filtering

 1 In the Details view (see page 140), select any header and click the **Down arrow** to the right-hand side

2 Select a box next to one or more ranges, and the items displayed are immediately restricted to that selection

3 You can select a second header – Size, for example – to apply additional filtering to the items displayed

Size   ⌄ Tags

☐ Medium (100 KB - 1 MB)

132 K ☐ Large (1 - 16 MB)

728 K ☐ Huge (16 - 128 MB)

4 The tick ✓ symbol on headers indicates that filtering is in effect, and the Address bar shows the attributes

> This PC > Pictures > Cyprus > Large (1 - 16 MB)   ⌄ ↻   Search Cyprus

📌 ^   Date   Type   Size   ✓ Tags

5 Filtering remains in effect even if you change folder views within the selected folder

Grouping

You can group the contents of a folder using the header ranges. You do not need to select the Details view.

1 Right-click an empty part of the folder area, select **Group by**, then select an attribute; e.g. **Size**

The right-click context menu also offers the **Sort by** option, so you can specify or change the sort sequence without switching to Details view.

2 The contents will be grouped, using the ranges for the attribute selected

143

Any sorting that was already in place will remain in effect. However, you can switch between **Ascending** and **Descending**.

3 Grouping is retained when you switch views (and when you revisit the folder after closing File Explorer)

Select **Group by** > **(None)** to remove grouping. Select **More...** to add other attributes. The new attributes will also appear in Details view.

4 You can regroup the folder contents by selecting another attribute. This will replace your original choice

Folder Options

You can change the appearance and the behavior of your folders by adjusting the folder settings.

 From the View tab on the Ribbon, click on the **Options** button and select the **Change folder and search options** link

2 Choose **Open each folder in its own window**, to keep multiple folders open at the same time

3 If you want items to open as they do on a web page, select **Single-click to open an item (point to select)**

4 Select the **View** tab to select options for how items appear in the File Explorer libraries

 Select **Apply** to try out the selected changes without closing the Folder Options, then **OK** to confirm

 Alternatively, select **Restore Defaults** then **Apply**, to reset all options to their default values

7 Managing Files and Folders

Folders can contain other folders as well as files, and Windows 10 treats them in very much the same way. Hence, operations such as moving, copying, deleting, and searching apply to files and to folders in a similar way. This chapter shows how to perform these tasks while working with File Explorer.

146 **Select Files and Folders**

148 **Copy or Move Files or Folders**

152 **File Conflicts**

153 **Open Files**

154 **Delete Files and Folders**

155 **The Recycle Bin**

158 **Create a Folder**

159 **Rename a File or Folder**

160 **Backtrack File Operations**

161 **File Properties**

162 **Search for Files and Folders**

163 **Compressed Folders**

Select Files and Folders

To process several files or folders, it is more efficient to select and process them as a group, rather than one by one:

Single file or folder

 Click the item to highlight it, then move, copy or delete it as required

Sequential files

 To highlight a range, click to select the first item, press and hold **Shift**, then click the last item

Adjacent block

 Click and hold, then drag out a box to cover the files you want selected. All the files in the rectangular area will be highlighted

Don't forget

Use the sorting, filtering and grouping options (see pages 141-143) to rearrange the files to make the selection easier.

Beware

You must start the selection box from an empty space in the folder. If you accidentally click a file or folder, you will drag that item, rather than create a box.

Non-adjacent files

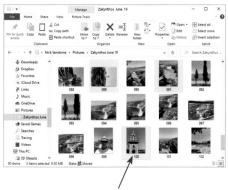

 To select several non-adjacent files, click one item, press and hold **Ctrl**, then click the subsequent items. As you select files, they are highlighted

Partial sequence

You can combine these techniques to select part of a range.

 Select a group of sequential files or an adjacent block of files (as described on the previous page)

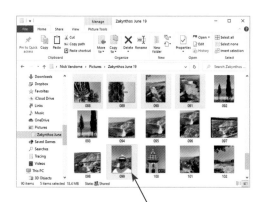

 Hold down **Ctrl** and click to deselect any files in the range that you do not want, and to select extra ones

All files and folders

To select all of the files (and folders) in the current folder, select the **Home** tab on the Ribbon and click on **Select All** or press **Ctrl** + **A**.

Hot tip

To deselect one file, click it while the **Ctrl** key is being held down. To deselect all of the files, click once anywhere in the folder outside of the selection area.

Beware

If you select a folder, you will also be selecting any files and folders that it may contain.

Copy or Move Files or Folders

You may wish to copy or move files and folders to another folder on the same drive, or to another drive. There are several ways to achieve this:

Drag, using the right mouse button

 Open File Explorer and the folder with the required files, then locate the destination in the Folders list in the Navigation pane

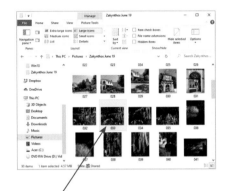

 In the folder contents, select the files and folders that you want to copy or move

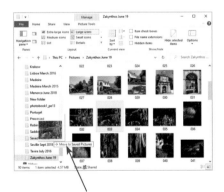

 Right-click any one of the selection, drag the files onto the destination folder or drive in the Folders list so it is highlighted and named, then release to display the menu

 Click the **Move here** or **Copy here** option as desired, and the files will be added to the destination folder

Copy here
Move here
Create shortcuts here

Cancel

Drag, using the left mouse button
In this case, default actions are applied with no intervening menu.

 1 Select the files and folders to be moved or copied

Hot tip

Open File Explorer and the source folder, then locate the destination in the Folders list in the Navigation pane, ready for moving or copying files and folders.

2 Use the left mouse button to drag the selection to the destination drive or folder in the Folders list – in this example, the removable USB storage drive (Flashdrive)

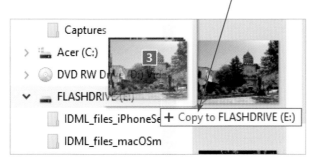

Hot tip

As you hover over a drive or folder in the Folders list in the Navigation pane, it expands to reveal the subfolders.

3 Press **Shift** to Move instead of Copy to another drive. Press **Ctrl** to Copy instead of Move to a folder on the same drive as the source folder

Don't forget

You will see a ✚ symbol if the file is going to be copied, or a ➡ if the file is going to be moved.

In summary

Drives	Drag	Drag + Shift	Drag + Ctrl
Same	Move	Move	Copy
Different	Copy	Move	Copy

...cont'd

Using Cut, Copy and Paste

1 Choose the files and folders you want to copy, and right-click within the selection

2 From the context menu, click **Copy** or **Cut** to move the selection

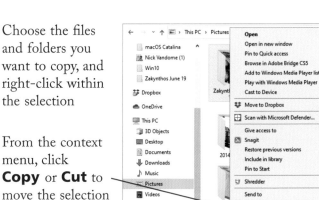

3 Move to the destination folder (or create a new one)

4 Right-click a blank area of the destination folder

5 Select **Paste** from the menu to complete the copy or move operation

Keyboard shortcuts

Cut, Copy and Paste options are also available as keyboard shortcuts. Select files and folders as above, but use these keys in place of the menu selections for Copy, Cut and Paste. There are also shortcuts to Undo an action or Redo an action.

Press this key	To do this
F1	Display Help
Ctrl+C	Copy the selected item
Ctrl+X	Cut the selected item
Ctrl+V	Paste the selected item
Ctrl+Z	Undo an action
Ctrl+Y	Redo an action

Burn to disc

If your computer has a CD or DVD recorder, you can copy files to a writable disc. This is usually termed "burning".

1 Insert a writable CD or DVD disc into the recorder drive (DVD/CD RW). Click on this pop-up

2 When the prompt appears, choose the option to **Burn files to disc** using File Explorer

DVD RW Drive (D:)

Choose what to do with blank DVDs.

Burn files to disc
File Explorer

Take no action

3 Make sure the CD/DVD is selected, and copy and paste files into the main window, drag files there to copy them to the disc, or

4 Select files within another File Explorer window and click on the **Burn to disc** button under the **Share** tab

You can use any of the methods described for copying or moving one or more files and folders.

File Conflicts

When you copy or move files from one folder to another, conflicts may arise. There may already be a file with the same name in the destination folder. To illustrate what may happen:

 Open a folder (e.g. **Documents** > **Win10** folder) and the USB flashdrive

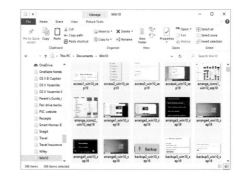

 Press **Ctrl** + **A** to select all of the files and drag them onto the flashdrive, to initiate a copy of them

Windows observes any conflicts – some files already exist, with identical size and date information. Select one of the options

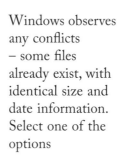

If you select the **Let me decide for each file** option, details will be displayed so you can view if one is newer than another. Click on the **Continue** button to confirm the decisions made

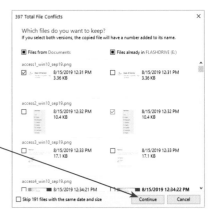

Hot tip

You can, of course, use the Copy and Paste options from the right-click menus, or use the equivalent keyboard shortcuts, and File Explorer will continue to check for possible conflicts.

Open Files

You can open a file using an associated app without first having to explicitly start that app. There are several ways to do this:

Default program

1 Double-click the file icon, or

2 Right-click the file and select **Open** from the menu, or

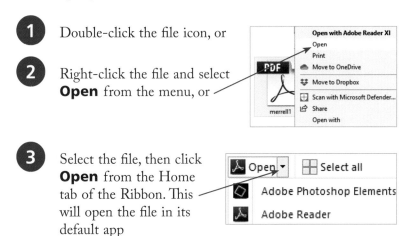

Default programs can also be set in **Settings** > **Apps** > **Default apps** or **Control Panel** > **Programs** > **Default programs** (in Category view).

3 Select the file, then click **Open** from the Home tab of the Ribbon. This will open the file in its default app

Alternative program (app)

You may have several apps that can open a particular file type. To use a different app than the default to open the file:

1 Right-click the file icon and select **Open with**. Pick an app from the list or click **Choose another app** to set a new default app

2 The same choices are presented when you select the Down arrow next to the **Open** button on the Ribbon in the folder window

Delete Files and Folders

When you want to remove files or folders, you use the same delete procedures – whatever drive or device the items are stored on.

1 Choose one or more files and folders, selected as described previously (see pages 146-147)

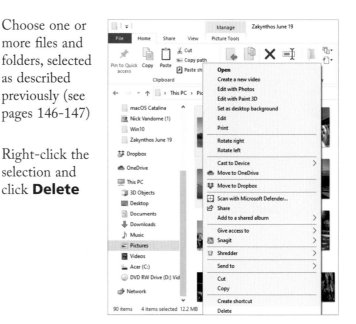

2 Right-click the selection and click **Delete**

3 Alternatively, click on the **Delete** button on the Ribbon, or click the arrow and select one of the options

If you choose to delete and then immediately realize that you have made a mistake deleting one or more files, right-click the folder area and select **Undo Delete** or press **Ctrl** + **Z**, to reverse the last operation. For hard disk items, you are also able to retrieve deleted files from the Recycle Bin, and this could be a substantial time later (unless you have emptied or bypassed the Recycle Bin – see pages 156-157).

The Recycle Bin

The Recycle Bin is, in effect, a folder on your hard disk that holds deleted files and folders. They are not physically removed from your hard disk (unless you empty the Recycle Bin or delete specific items from within the Recycle Bin itself). They will remain there until the Recycle Bin fills up, at which time the oldest deleted files may finally be removed.

The Recycle Bin, therefore, provides a safety net for files and folders you may delete by mistake, and allows you to easily retrieve them, even at a later date.

Restoring files

 Double-click on the **Recycle Bin** icon from the Desktop or in the Navigation pane

To see where the Recycle Bin is located, right-click in a clear area of the **Navigation pane** and select **Show all folders**.

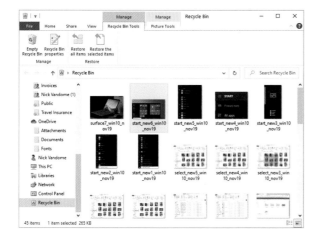

 Select the **Restore all items** button, or select a file and the button changes to **Restore the selected items**

A restored folder will include all the files and subfolders that it held when it was originally deleted.

...cont'd

Permanently erase files

You may want to explicitly delete particular files, perhaps for reasons of privacy and confidentiality.

 Open the Recycle Bin

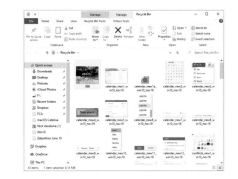

You do not have to worry about the space used in the Recycle Bin. Windows keeps track and removes the oldest deleted entries when the maximum allowed space – typically 10% of the drive – has been used.

 Select the relevant files and folders, then select **Delete** from the one of the menus (or press the **Delete** key)

 Select **Yes**, to confirm that you want to permanently delete these files (completely remove them from the hard disk)

Empty the Recycle Bin

If desired, you can remove all of the contents of the Recycle Bin from the hard disk:

Right-click the Recycle Bin icon and select **Empty Recycle Bin**, to remove all of the files and folders without it being open.

Open
Empty Recycle Bin
Pin to Start
Create shortcut
Rename
Properties

1 With the Recycle Bin open, select the **Empty Recycle Bin** button

2 Press **Yes** to confirm the permanent deletion

The Recycle Bin icon changes from full to empty, to illustrate the change.

Bypass the Recycle Bin

If you want to prevent particular deleted files from being stored in the Recycle Bin:

1 From their original location, select the files and folders, right-click the selection, but this time hold down the **Shift** key as you select **Delete**

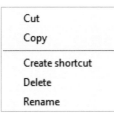

You could also just press the **Delete** key on the keyboard to delete items, or **Shift** + the **Delete** key to delete items permanently.

2 Confirm that you want to permanently delete the selected item or items. "Permanent" means that no copy will be kept

Deactivate (or resize) the Recycle Bin

You can tell Windows to always bypass the Recycle Bin:

1 Right-click the Recycle Bin icon, then select **Properties** from the menu

2 Note the space available in the Recycle Bin location (free space on hard disk)

3 Adjust the maximum size allowed, to resize the Recycle Bin

4 Click the button labeled **Don't move files to the Recycle Bin. Remove files immediately when deleted**, to always bypass the Recycle Bin

Take extra care when selecting files and folders if you are bypassing the Recycle Bin, since you will have no recovery options.

157

Create a Folder

You can create a new folder in a drive, folder or on the Desktop:

 1 Right-click an empty part of the folder window, select **New** and then **Folder** (or select the **New folder** button on the Ribbon)

 2 Overtype the default name New Folder; e.g. type *Articles*, and press **Enter**

You can also create a new file in a standard format for use with one of the apps installed on your computer:

1 Right-click an empty part of the folder, select **New**, and choose the specific file type; e.g. Text Document file

 2 Overtype the file name provided, and press **Enter**

Rename a File or Folder

You can rename a file or folder at any time, by simply editing the current name:

 Right-click the file/folder, then click **Rename**, or select the icon and click on the icon name (or select the **Rename** button on the Ribbon)

Open
Scan with Windows Defender...
Share
Open with...
Give access to ▸
Shredder ▸
Restore previous versions
Send to ▸
Cut
Copy
Create shortcut
Delete
Rename

 Either way, the current name will be highlighted. Type a name to delete and replace the current name, or press the arrow keys to position the typing cursor and edit the existing name:

 Press **Enter** or click elsewhere to confirm the new name

Preserving file types

When you have file extensions revealed and you create or rename a file or folder, only the name itself, not the file type, will be highlighted. This avoids accidental changes of type.

   Genealogy.txt

Use the same method to rename icons on the Desktop. You can even rename the Recycle Bin.

You must always provide a non-blank file name, and you should avoid special characters such as quote marks, question marks and periods/full stops.

You can change the file type (extension), but you will be warned that this may make the file unusable.

Hot tip

Undo mistakes as soon as possible, since you would have to undo subsequent operations first. Also, only a limited amount of undo history is maintained.

Don't forget

The Undo command that is offered changes depending on which operation was being performed at the time.

Don't forget

If you go back too far, right-click the folder and select the available Redo operation; e.g. Redo Rename.

Beware

Undo commands do not work on permanently deleted files.

Backtrack File Operations

If you accidentally delete, rename, copy or move the wrong file or folder, you can undo (reverse) the last operation and preceding operations, to get back to where you started. For example:

 Right-click the folder area and select the **Undo Rename** command that is displayed

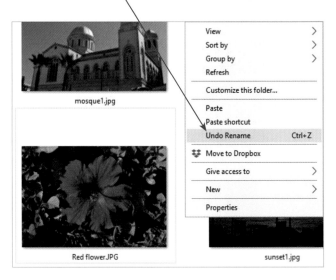

 Right-click again, and this time there is an **Undo Delete** command for you to select

3 Now you will have reversed the last two operations, putting the folder and files back as they were before the changes

File Properties

Every file (and every folder) has information that can be displayed in the Properties dialog box. To display this:

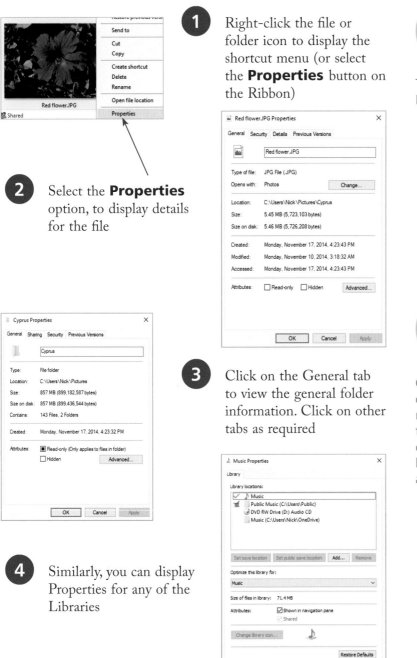

1 Right-click the file or folder icon to display the shortcut menu (or select the **Properties** button on the Ribbon)

2 Select the **Properties** option, to display details for the file

3 Click on the General tab to view the general folder information. Click on other tabs as required

4 Similarly, you can display Properties for any of the Libraries

The purpose of the Properties dialog box is:
• to display details;
• to change settings for the selected file or folder.

Click **Security** and the other tabs, to display more information about the file or folder, and click the **Advanced...** button for additional attributes.

Search for Files and Folders

If you are not quite sure where exactly you stored a file, or what the full name is, the File Explorer Search box may be the answer.

 Open a location, e.g. Documents, click in the Search box and start typing a word from the file; e.g. *Nick*

Hot tip

Open the library or folder that is most likely to hold the file you want, then click in the Search box to initiate a search, looking at file names and content limited to that folder and its subfolders.

Don't forget

Some files contain the search words in the file names, while others contain the words within the textual content.

2 If that produces too many files, start typing another word that might help limit the number of matches; e.g. *Vandome*

Hot tip

For an attached hard drive, you may be offered the option to **Click to add to index**, and thereby speed up future searches. Indexing is the process of the Search facility storing the words that can be searched over.

Hot tip

You can also use Cortana to search for files and folders (see pages 65-66).

3 If the location is a drive rather than a library, its contents may not be indexed, so the search may take longer

Compressed Folders

This feature allows you to save disk space by compressing files and folders, while allowing them to be treated as normal by Windows 10.

Create a compressed folder

 Right-click an empty portion of the folder window and select **New > Compressed (zipped) Folder**

 A compressed folder is created, with the default name New Compressed (zipped) Folder.zip

3 Rename it (see page 159). You can also open, move, or delete it just like any other folder

New Compressed (zipped) Folder.zip

Add files or folders to a compressed folder

1 Drag files or folders onto a compressed folder and they will automatically be compressed and stored there

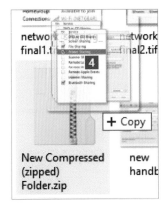

New Compressed (zipped) Folder.zip

Rename it (see page 159).

Hot tip

Compressed folders are distinguished from other folders by a zipper on the folder icon. They are compatible with other zip archive apps, such as WinZip.

163

Don't forget

To create a compressed folder and copy a file into it at the same time: right-click a file in File Explorer, select **Send to > Compressed (zipped) folder**. The new compressed folder has the same file name, but with a file extension of .zip.

...cont'd

Compressed item Properties

 Double-click the compressed folder and select any file to see the compressed size versus the original size

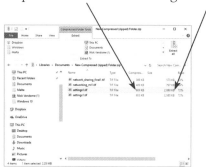

Extract files and folders

 Open the compressed folder, drag files and folders onto a normal folder and they will be decompressed. The compressed version still remains in the compressed folder, unless you hold the Shift key as you drag (i.e. Move)

Extract all

 To extract all of the files and folders from a compressed folder, right-click it and then click on **Extract all** or select it from the Extract section on the Ribbon

Extract all

 Accept or edit the target folder and click **Extract**. The files and folders are decompressed and transferred

Hot tip

If the folder specified does not exist, it will be created automatically.

8 Digital Lifestyle

Windows 10 covers a range of entertainment with the Photos, Groove Music and Movies & TV apps. This chapter shows how to work with these apps, and also the online OneDrive function for backing up content.

166   Using OneDrive

169   OneDrive Settings

170   Viewing Photos

172   Editing Photos

174   Groove Music

175   Playing Music

176   Viewing Movies and TV

178   Using Paint 3D

179   Gaming with Windows 10

OneDrive has a **Personal Vault** folder that has added levels of security for storing your most sensitive and important documents and photos. It requires an extra level of security to access the Personal Vault; e.g. a PIN code or a code that is sent to you via email or text message. The Personal Vault can be accessed from any of the OneDrive interfaces. This is a new feature in the Windows 10 November 2019 Update.

Click on these buttons on the right-hand side of the OneDrive toolbar in Step 2 (i.e. when you are signed in to the web version of OneDrive) to, from left to right: sort the content; display it as a grid; or view its details.

Using OneDrive

Cloud computing is now a mainstream part of our online experience. This involves saving content to an online server connected to the service that you are using – i.e. through your Microsoft Account. You can then access this content from any computer or mobile device using your account login details, and also share it with other people by giving them access to your Cloud service. It can also be used to back up your files, in case they get corrupted or damaged on your PC.

The Cloud service with Windows 10 is known as OneDrive, and you can use it with a Microsoft Account. It consists of the OneDrive folder in the File Explorer, the OneDrive app, and the online OneDrive website. Content added to any of the elements will be available in the others. To use them:

1 Click on the **OneDrive** folder in the File Explorer to view its contents. Or, click on this button on the Start menu

2 Download the OneDrive app from the Microsoft Store and click on this icon on the Start menu to open it. It should display the same items as in the OneDrive folder in the File Explorer

...cont'd

3 To view the contents of
OneDrive online, go to
the website at **onedrive.
live.com** and sign in
with your Microsoft
Account details. Your
OneDrive content is
the same as in your
OneDrive folder on your computer

Your OneDrive folder
can be pinned to the
Quick access section
in File Explorer. To do
this, right-click on the
OneDrive icon in File
Explorer and click on
Pin to Quick access.

Files and folders can be added to OneDrive from any of the three
elements:

Adding items to OneDrive in File Explorer

1 In File Explorer, the OneDrive
folder is located underneath
Quick access (and any other
folders that have been added)

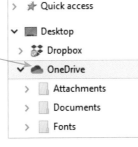

By default, you get 5GB
of free OneDrive storage
space with Windows 10
(the free allowance was
reduced from 15GB in
July 2016). This is an
excellent way to back
up your important
documents, since they
are stored away from
your computer. For
up-to-date information
on plan allowances and
pricing, visit **https://
onedrive.live.com/
about/plans/**

2 Click on the
OneDrive folder to
view its contents

3 Add files to the
OneDrive folder by
dragging and dropping
them from another
folder, or by using
Copy and Paste

...cont'd

Adding items to the OneDrive app

1. Open the OneDrive app and click on the **Upload** button

2. Select whether to upload **Files** or a **Folder** from your computer

3. Navigate to the required item in File Explorer, select it, and click on the **Select Folder** button to add it to your OneDrive folder

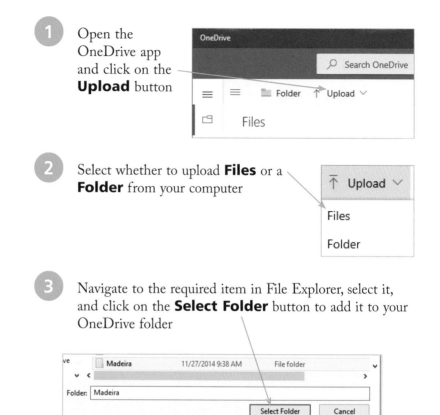

Adding items to OneDrive online

1. Access your online OneDrive account and click on the **Upload** button

2. Select whether to upload **Files** or a **Folder** and navigate to the required items as above

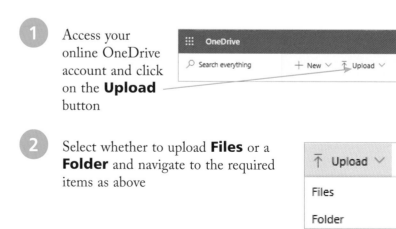

OneDrive Settings

A range of settings can be applied to OneDrive, including adding and syncing folders. To do this:

1 Right-click on the OneDrive icon on the Notification area of the Taskbar and click on **Settings**

Settings

2 Click on the **Settings** tab for options for starting OneDrive when you sign in, and for receiving notifications if other people share items to your OneDrive

Microsoft OneDrive   ✕

Settings Account Backup Network Office About

General
☑ Start OneDrive automatically when I sign in to Windows
☑ Automatically pause sync when this device is in battery saver mode
☑ Automatically pause sync when this device is on a metered network
☐ Let me use OneDrive to fetch any of my files on this PC
  More info

Notifications
☑ Display notifications when people share with me or edit my shared files
☑ Notify me when many files are deleted in the cloud
☑ Warn me before removing files from the cloud
☑ Notify me when sync is auto-paused

Files On-Demand
☑ Save space and download files as you use them
  More info

                                              OK   Cancel

If the OneDrive icon is not visible on the Taskbar, turn it **On** in **Settings** > **Personalization** > **Taskbar** > **Select which icons appear on the taskbar**, under the **Notification area** heading.

169

3 Click on the **Account** tab and click on the **Choose folders** button to select the folder from your computer that you want to sync with your OneDrive account

Microsoft OneDrive   ✕

Settings Account Backup Network Office About

OneDrive (nickvandome@gmail.com)
32 MB of 5.0 GB cloud storage used   [Add an account]
Get more storage   Unlink this PC

Choose folders
Folders you choose will be available on this PC.   [Choose folders]

                                              OK   Cancel

The Account section can also be used to unlink your PC so that files on your computer are not synced with the online OneDrive. Click on the **Unlink this PC** option to do this.

4 Click on the **OK** button to apply any changes to the OneDrive settings

Viewing Photos

The Photos app can be used to manage and edit your photos, including those stored in your **Pictures** Library. To do this:

Hot tip

To import photos into the Photos app, click on this button

on the top toolbar and select the location from where you want to import the photos. This can be a folder on your own computer; a camera or flashdrive attached with a USB cable; or a memory card from a camera inserted into a card reader.

Don't forget

Click on the **Folders** button to view photos that have been taken with your computer's camera (or copied into this folder from another location).

1 Click on the **Photos** app on the **Start menu**

2 The main categories are at the left-hand side of the screen, on the top toolbar

Collection   Albums   People   Folders

3 Other options are at the right-hand side of the toolbar, including searching photos, selecting an item(s) and importing photos

4 Click on the **Collection** button to view all of the photos in the Photos app, arranged by date. Scroll up and down to view the photos

5 Click on the **Albums** button to view photos from specific albums

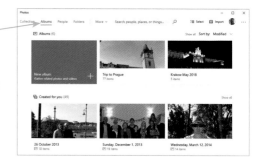

6 Within the Albums section, double-click on an album to view its contents. The first photo is also displayed as a banner at the top of the album

Don't forget

Albums can include photos and videos.

7 Double-click on a photo within an album, or collection, to view it at full size. Move the cursor over the photo and click on the left and right arrows (if available) to move through an album or collection

Hot tip

Photos within either a collection or an album in the Photos app can be selected and then shared with other people in various ways, or deleted. To do this: in Collections or an open Album, click on the **Select** button on the top toolbar. Click in the box in the top-right corner to select a photo or photos. Click on the **Share** button to share the selected photo(s).

Editing Photos

In Windows 10, the Photos app has a range of editing functions so that you can improve and enhance your photos. To use these:

 Open a photo at full size

The
Draw Draw
button   Add an artistic touch
is available from the Edit
& Create drop-down
menu. Click on this to
access pen options for
drawing directly on
an image. Click on the
Save button to save
a copy of the image,
or click on the cross to
discard changes.

 Click on the **Edit & Create** button on the top toolbar and click on the **Edit** button to access additional editing options. Scroll up and down the right-hand panel to view the editing options

3 By default, the **Crop & rotate** option is opened in Step 2. This can be used to crop the current photo or rotate it in a variety of ways, such as straightening, or flipping horizontally or vertically

Most photos benefit from some degree of cropping, so that the main subject is given greater prominence by removing unwanted items in the background.

4 Click on the **Filters** button on the top toolbar to apply filter effects. Click an effect to apply it. Click on the **Enhance your photo** option to auto-enhance the colors in the photo

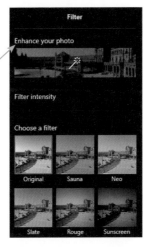

5 Click on the **Adjustments** button on the top toolbar to apply a range of color adjustments. Click next to an adjustment category to view more options. Drag the sliders to apply the amount of the editing option, as required

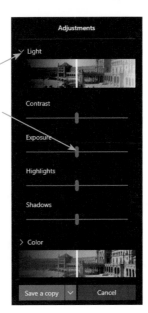

Click on the **Save a copy** button at the bottom of the editing panels to save a copy of an edited image, without changing the original. Click on the down-pointing arrow to access an option to **Save** the edited image, which now becomes the original.

173

Groove Music

The Groove Music app is used to access music that you have added to your computer. To use it:

1 Click on the **Groove Music** app on the Start menu

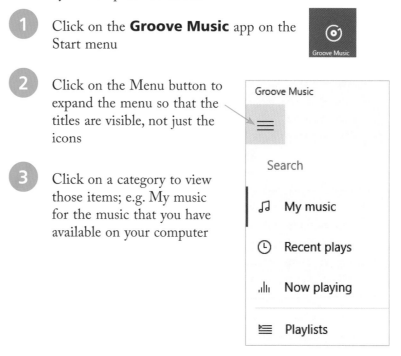

2 Click on the Menu button to expand the menu so that the titles are visible, not just the icons

3 Click on a category to view those items; e.g. My music for the music that you have available on your computer

4 The items within the selected category are displayed. Use the tabs on the top toolbar to view items according to these categories

Playing Music

Playing your own music

Music that has been added to your computer can be played through the Groove Music app, and you can automatically specify new music to be included when it is added. To do this:

1 Open the Groove Music app and click on the **My music** button

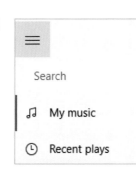

2 Click on Songs, Artists or Albums tabs, as shown in Step 4 on the previous page, to view the items within each category

3 Click on an item to access it

4 Click on a track or album to start playing it

5 Use these buttons above to, from left to right: shuffle the available tracks; go to the start of a track; pause/play a track; go to the end of a track; repeat a track; or change or mute the volume

You can also add music to the Groove Music app from the Library that you have stored in your OneDrive folder.

When a folder is added to the Music Library, any music that is copied here will be displayed by the Groove Music app.

The Spotify app can be used to stream music using Windows 10. This can be downloaded directly from the Groove Music app.

Viewing Movies and TV

For movie and TV lovers, the Movies & TV app can be used to download and watch your favorite movies and shows. It connects to the Microsoft Store from where you can preview and buy a large range of content:

1 Click on the **Movies & TV** app on the Start menu

2 The Microsoft Store opens at the **Explore** section for viewing available items

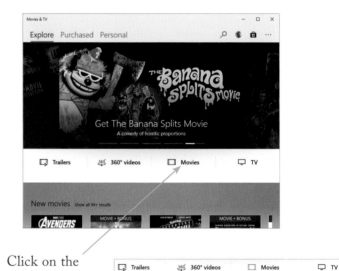

Click on the **Purchased** button in Step 2 to view all of the items you have bought.

3 Click on the **Movies** (or **TV**) button to view the available items

4 Click on an item to see more information, view a preview clip, or buy, rent, or download the movie

Movies and TV shows can be streamed (viewed from the computer server where the item is stored, rather than downloading it) if you have a fast internet connection. They can also be downloaded to a single device so that they can be viewed while you are offline.

...cont'd

 Click on the **Trailers** button to view previews of movies

 Click on an item to view its trailer

7 The trailer plays in the Movies & TV window

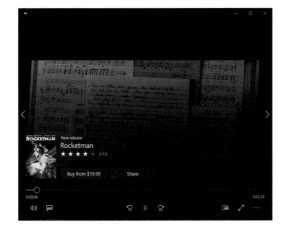

The interface for viewing a trailer is the same as for viewing a movie or TV show that has been bought or rented. Click on the main window to access the control buttons at the bottom of the screen.

8 Click on the **Personal** button on the top toolbar to view your own videos that have

Personal

been added to your computer. Items from the **Video** folders are displayed, and new folders can be added, using the **Add folders** button

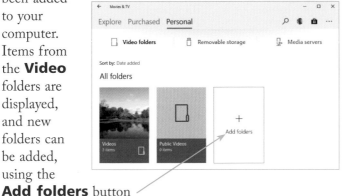

177

Using Paint 3D

Windows 10 caters for a wide range of 3D use, and one of the most significant is the Paint 3D app that can be used to create your own 3D pictures using graphics and text, and also to import ones from other places.

Around Paint 3D

In some ways, Paint 3D is an extension of the Windows Paint app. However, it has a much greater array of features, and brings the creation of 3D pictures within reach of anyone. To get started with creating 3D pictures:

 Click on the **Paint 3D** app

 Click on the **New** button to create a new blank project

 The Paint 3D workspace includes the canvas (the white square in the middle), the background, the tools for creating content, and the tools palette (at the right-hand side)

 Click on the **Brushes** button on the top toolbar to select brush types and colors

Click on the **3D objects** button on the top toolbar to add 3D shapes

Click on the **Stickers** button on the top toolbar to add 3D graphics

Click on the **Text** button on the top toolbar to add 3D text effects

Click on the **Effects** button on the top toolbar to add background effects

Gaming with Windows 10

Game players are well catered for in Windows 10, with the Xbox Console app for playing games and interacting with other gamers. To play games with the Windows 10:

 Click on the **Start** button and click on the **Xbox Console Companion** app

 Click on the **Home** button to view the Xbox Homepage. This contains the **Toolbar** (down the left-hand side), the **Activity feed** (in

the middle panel) and the options for joining clubs and connecting with other gamers (in the right-hand panel)

You have to be signed in with your Microsoft Account in order to use the Xbox Console app and all of its features.

Click on the **My games** button to view system games or those that you have downloaded from the Microsoft Store

Click on the **Play** button next to a game in Step 3 to open it and start playing it.

Click on the **Achievements** button to view your scores from games you have played, and compare them with other gamers

...cont'd

Don't forget

Click on this button on the toolbar to view any screenshots or videos that you have captured of the games you have played. This can be done with the **Game Bar**, which can be opened by pressing **WinKey** + **G**.

Don't forget

Click on this button on the toolbar to view **Trending** topics from within the gaming community.

Don't forget

Using the Xbox Console Companion app with Windows 10 can be a very interactive experience in terms of communicating with and playing with other gamers. However, it can also be used to play games on your own.

5 Click on the **Clubs** button to view details of online game playing clubs. This is where you can join up with other players, to compare scores and also play online games against other players (multiplayer games)

6 In the right-hand panel, click on the **Friends list** button to view friends that you have added (this can be done by searching for them through the Xbox app in the **Find people or clubs** box, or by linking to them via Facebook)

7 Click on the **Parties** button to create a group of multiplayer gamers, who can all play together

8 Click on the **Messages** button to send messages to people in your groups and clubs, and also view messages you have received

9 Click on the **Activity alerts** button to view any activity in relation to messages you have sent or comments you have made

9 Microsoft Edge Browser

The Microsoft Edge browser is fast and responsive, and has a range of impressive features. This chapter looks at how to use the Edge browser to open web pages, use tabs, bookmarks and reading lists, and add notes and annotations to pages.

182 About the Edge Browser

183 Smart Address Bar

184 Setting a Homepage

185 Using Tabs

188 Bookmarking Web Pages

189 Adding Notes to Web Pages

191 Organizing with the Hub

192 Reading List

193 Reading View

194 More Options

About the Edge Browser

The web browser Internet Explorer (IE) has been synonymous with Microsoft for almost as long as the Windows operating system. Introduced in 1995, shortly after Windows 95, it was the default browser for a generation of web users. However, as with most technologies, the relentless march of time caught up with IE, and although it is still included with Windows 10, the preferred browser is designed specifically for the digital mobile age. It is called Microsoft Edge, and adapts easily to whichever environment it is operating in: desktop, tablet or phone.

The Microsoft Edge browser has a number of performance and speed enhancements compared with IE, and it also recognizes that modern web users want a lot more from their browser than simply being able to look at web pages. It includes a function for drawing on and annotating web pages that can then be sent to other people as screenshots.

There is also a Hub where you can store all of your favorite web pages, downloads and pages that you have selected to read at a later date (which can be when you are offline if required).

Click on this icon from the **Taskbar** or the **Start** menu to open the Microsoft Edge browser at the default Start page.

Beware

For details about connecting to a network, and the internet, see page 209.

Don't forget

Internet Explorer can still be used with Windows 10. You can find it under Windows Accessories on the Start menu.

Don't forget

The Start page also displays news information.

Hot tip

The Start page can be replaced by your own specific Homepage – see page 184 for details.

Back/forward buttons   Refresh   Hub button   Toolbar buttons

More options (Menu button)

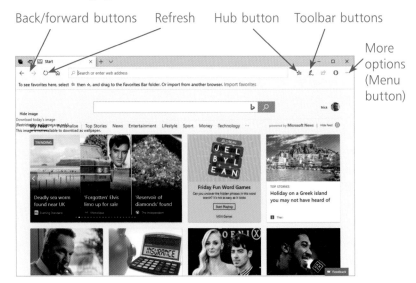

Smart Address Bar

Smart address bars are now a familiar feature in a lot of modern browsers, and Microsoft Edge is no different. This can be used to enter a specific web address to open that page, or use it to search for a word or phrase. To use the smart address bar:

1 Click anywhere in the address box at the top of a web page

| 🗐 | 🗗 | 🔲 Start | × | + | ∨ |

← → ↻ ⌂   🔍 Search or enter web address

The personal digital assistant, Cortana, can also be used to open web pages, by asking it to open a specific page. The page will be opened in Microsoft Edge.

2 Start typing a word or website address. As you type, options appear below the address bar. Click on a web page address to open that website

> ineasysteps
>
> ineasysteps.**com**
>
> **in easy steps**
>
> **in easy steps pdf**
>
> **in easy steps books**
>
> **in easy steps ltd**
>
> **in easy steps limited**
>
> **in easy steps publishing**
>
> **in easy steps book series**

3 Click on one of the options with a magnifying glass next to it to view the search result for that item

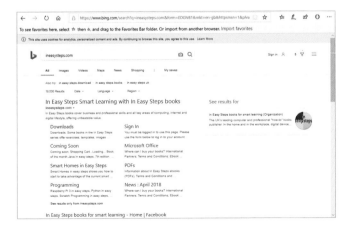

The Microsoft Edge browser has a Homepage button on the top toolbar. (If you can't see this, go to the **Settings** button in Step 2. Click on the **General** button in the left-hand sidebar and click the **Show the home button** option **On**.)

Within the settings for Microsoft Edge there is an option for importing Favorites from another web browser. To do this, click on the **Import or export** button below the **Transfer favorites and other info** heading in Step 4, select the required browser and click on the **Import** button.

If a specific Homepage is assigned, the Start page as shown on page 182 will not be displayed.

Setting a Homepage

By default, Microsoft Edge opens at its own Start page. This may not be ideal for most users, who will want to set their own Homepage that appears when Microsoft Edge is launched.

1 Click on this button on the top toolbar to access the menu options

2 Click on the **Settings** button

Settings

3 Click on the **General** button in the left-hand sidebar

4 Scroll down the page to access the **Open Microsoft Edge with** option. By default, the **Start page** is selected as the opening page

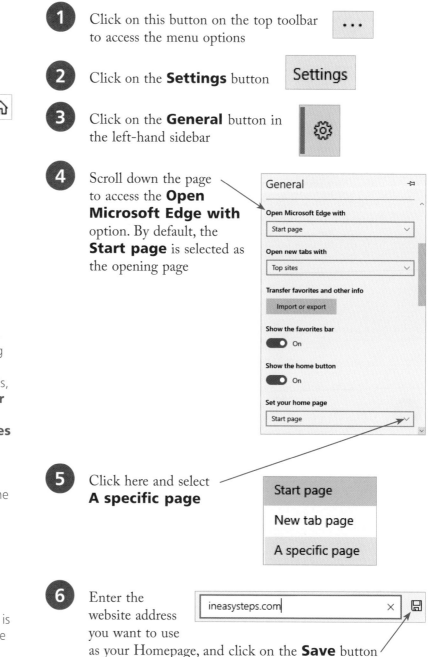

5 Click here and select **A specific page**

Start page

New tab page

A specific page

6 Enter the website address you want to use as your Homepage, and click on the **Save** button

ineasysteps.com

Using Tabs

Being able to open several web pages at the same time in different tabs is now a common feature of web browsers. To do this with Microsoft Edge:

 1 Click on this button at the top of the Microsoft Edge window

 Welcome to Windows

 2 Pages can be opened in new tabs using the smart address bar or the list of **Top sites** that appears below it

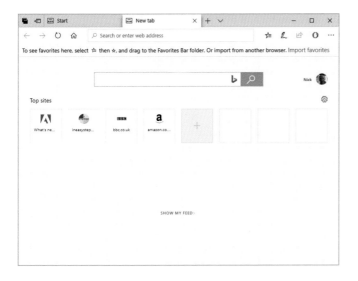

 3 All open tabs are displayed at the top of the window. Click and hold on a tab to drag it into a new position

Hot tip

The Start page for new tabs, as displayed in Step 2, can be changed if required. To do this, open the Microsoft Edge Settings as shown on the previous page and change the selection under the **Open new tabs with** heading.

NEW

Customized themes can be applied to pages, whether they are existing ones, or new tabs. To do this, access **Settings > General** as shown on the previous page and click in the **Choose a theme box**. The options are for **Light** or **Dark**. This is a new feature in the Windows 10 November 2019 Update.

...cont'd

Tab previews

If there are a large number of tabs open it can be hard to remember exactly what is in each one. This is addressed in the Edge browser through the tab previews function. To use this:

1 All open tabs are shown at the top of the browser, with the current active tab colored light gray

2 Move the mouse cursor over one of the inactive tabs to view a preview of the content within it

3 Click on this button next to the New Tab button to view thumbnails of all of the current tabs

4 Thumbnails of all of the current tabs are displayed. Click on one to view it, or click on this button to close the preview panel

Hot tip

Individual tabs can be muted if they are playing media, such as music or a video. If media is playing in a tab a small speaker icon is displayed.

Click on the speaker to mute the tab (a cross appears next to the icon).

Set aside tabs

To avoid the Edge browser window becoming too cluttered with open tabs at the top of it, it is possible to set aside the current tabs so that they are stored together, but not along the top of the browser window. To do this:

1 All open tabs are shown at the top of the browser

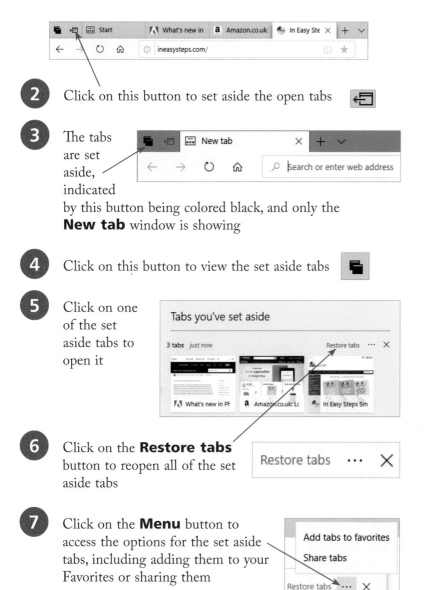

2 Click on this button to set aside the open tabs

3 The tabs are set aside, indicated by this button being colored black, and only the **New tab** window is showing

4 Click on this button to view the set aside tabs

5 Click on one of the set aside tabs to open it

6 Click on the **Restore tabs** button to reopen all of the set aside tabs

7 Click on the **Menu** button to access the options for the set aside tabs, including adding them to your Favorites or sharing them

Web pages can be pinned to the Start menu or the Taskbar. To do this, select the Menu button at the right-hand side of the browser toolbar and select **Pin this page to the taskbar**. Click on the **More tools** button to access the options for pinning the page to the Start menu. This is a new feature in the Windows 10 November 2019 Update.

Bookmarking Web Pages

Your favorite web pages can be bookmarked so that you can access them with one click from the Hub area, rather than having to enter the web address each time. To do this:

 Open the web page that you want to bookmark

 Click on this button on the toolbar

The Favorites bar can be displayed underneath the Address bar by opening the Microsoft Edge **Settings** (see page 184) and dragging the **Show the favorites bar** button **On**.

 Click on the **Favorites** button

 Enter a name for the Favorite and where you want it to be saved to

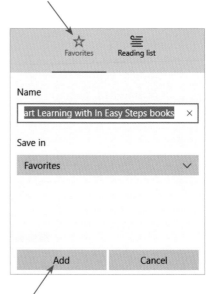

Name

art Learning with In Easy Steps books ✕

Save in

Favorites ⌄

Add   Cancel

 Click on the **Add** button

 The star button turns yellow, indicating that the web page has been added as a Favorite

Click on this button to access your Favorites (see page 191)

Adding Notes to Web Pages

One of the innovations in the Microsoft Edge browser is the ability to draw on and annotate web pages. This can be useful to highlight parts of a web page or add your own comments and views, which can then be sent to other people. To add notes:

 Open a web page to which you want to add a note or draw on, and click on this button on the toolbar of the Microsoft Edge browser

Don't forget

Click on this button on the Notes toolbar to create a web clipping. This is an area of a web page that is selected by dragging over it to make the selection.

 Click on one of the pen options

 Make selections for the pen style, including color and size

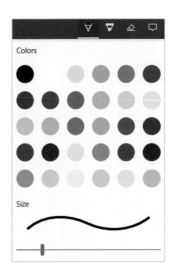

Don't forget

Click on this button on the Notes toolbar to **Save** a web note or clipping. These can then be accessed from the Favorites section of Microsoft Edge (see page 191).

...cont'd

4 Click and drag on the web page to draw over it

5 Click on the eraser icon and drag over any items that you have drawn to remove them, or part of them

6 Click on the text icon to add your own text

7 Drag over the web page to create a text box

8 Type the text that you want displayed on the web page

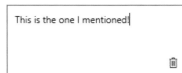

This is the one I mentioned!

9 Click and drag here on a text box to move its position

Beware

Several notes can be added to a web page, but it can begin to look a bit cluttered if there are too many.

190

Organizing with the Hub

The Hub is the area where you can store a variety of items for the Microsoft Edge browser; from your favorite web pages to pages that you want to read offline at a later date. To use the Hub:

1 Click on this button to open the Hub

2 Click on this button to view your **Favorites**. Click on one to go to that page

3 Click on this button to view your **Reading list** of pages that you have saved to read offline, or at a later date (see page 192 for details)

4 Click on this button to view your web browsing **History**

5 Click on **Clear history** to delete the browsing history

6 Click on this button to view items that you have downloaded from the web, such as PDF documents or images

Hot tip

Although the Books app is no longer supported by Microsoft, the Books button in the Hub can be used to access the Microsoft Store for accessing ebooks options.

Reading List

With some web pages you may want to save the content so that you can read it at a later date. If you make the page a Favorite, the content could change the next time you look at it. Instead, you can add the page to your Reading list to ensure that you can read the same content. Also, you have the advantage of being able to access the items in your Reading list when you are offline and not connected to the internet. To do this:

 Open the web page that you want to add to the Reading list

 Click on this button on the Edge toolbar

 Click on the **Reading list** button

Name

Space agencies aim to deliver rocks f   ×

Add   Cancel

 Enter a name for the item and click on the **Add** button

5 Click on the **Reading list** button within the Hub to access and view your Reading list items

Hot tip

The Reading list is an excellent option if you are traveling and do not have internet access. You can save numerous articles in the Reading list and access them even when you are offline.

Reading View

Modern web pages contain a lot more items than just text and pictures: video clips, pop-up ads, banners, and more contribute to the multimedia effect on many web pages. At times this additional content can enhance the page, but a lot of the time it is a distraction. If you want to just concentrate on the main item on a web page you can do this with the Reading view function:

 1 Open the web page that you want to view in Reading view

Not all web pages support the Reading view functionality. If it is not supported, the button in Step 2 will be grayed out.

2 Click on this button on the Microsoft Edge toolbar

3 The text and pictures are presented on a new page, with any additional content removed

On pages where Reading view is available (but not selected), select the **Print** button as shown in Step 5 on the next page and select **On** in the **Clutter-free printing** box to print the Reading view text. This is a new feature in the Windows 10 November 2019 Update.

 4 Click on this button again to return to the standard page view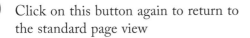

More Options

There is no traditional menu bar in Microsoft Edge, but more options can be accessed from the right-hand toolbar:

The full range of Microsoft Edge **Settings** can be accessed from the **Settings** button. This includes categories for **General**, **Privacy & security**, **Passwords & autofill** and **Advanced**. These categories can be accessed from the buttons in the left-hand sidebar of the Settings.

194

1 Click on this button to access the menu options

2 Click here to open a new browsing window, or a **New InPrivate window** that does not record any of your browsing history

🔲 New window	Ctrl+N
🔳 New InPrivate window	Ctrl+Shift+P
Zoom — 80% + ⤢	
⭐ Favorites	Ctrl+I
≣ Reading list	Ctrl+M
📖 Books	Ctrl+Shift+U
🕓 History	Ctrl+H
↓ Downloads	Ctrl+J
⚙ Extensions	
Show in toolbar	>
🖶 Print	Ctrl+P
🔍 Find on page	Ctrl+F
A⁹ Read aloud	Ctrl+Shift+G
📌 Pin this page to the taskbar	
More tools	>
⚙ Settings	

3 Click on the **Zoom** button to increase or decrease the magnification of the page being viewed

4 Click on the **Find on page** button to search for a specific word or phrase on the web page

5 Click on the **Print** button to print the current web page

10 Keeping in Touch

This chapter looks at communicating via the Mail, People, Skype and Calendar apps.

196 Setting Up Mail

198 Working with Mail

200 Chatting with Skype

202 Finding People

204 Using the Calendar

Setting Up Mail

Email has become an essential part of everyday life, both socially and in the business world. Windows 10 accommodates this with the Mail app. This can be used to link to online services such as Gmail and Outlook (the renamed version of Hotmail), and also other email accounts. To set up an email account with Mail:

1 Click on the **Mail** app on the Start menu

2 Click on the **Accounts** button

3 Click on the **Add account** button

Hot tip

The **Other account** option in Step 4 can be used to add a non-webmail account. This is usually a POP3 or an IMAP account, and you will need your email address, username, password, and usually the incoming and outgoing email servers. If you do not know these, they should be supplied by your email provider. They should also be available in the account settings of the email account you want to add to the Mail app.

4 Select the type of account to which you want to link via the Mail app. This can be an online email account that you have already set up

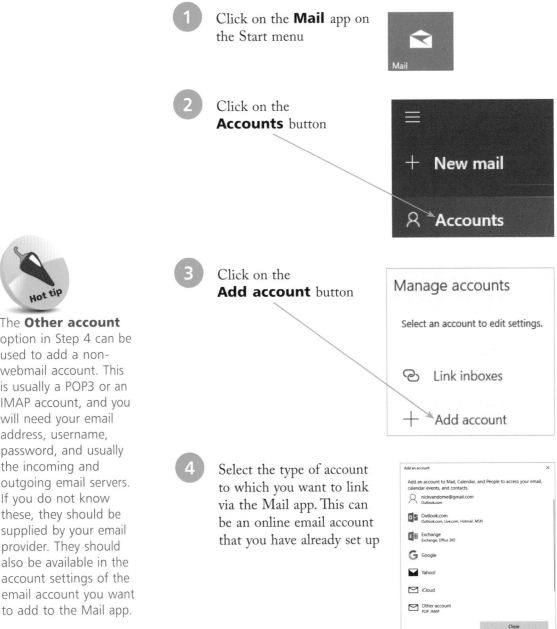

5 Enter your current sign-in details for the selected email account and click on the **Sign in** button

You can add more than one account to the Mail app. If you do this, you will be able to select the different accounts to view within Mail.

6 Once it has been connected, the details of the account are shown under the Mail button, including

the mailboxes within the account. Click on the **Accounts** button to view all linked accounts

7 The list of emails appears in the main panel. Double-click on an email to view it at full size

Click on this button at the top of the left-hand toolbar to expand and collapse the menu items, with their text descriptions.

197

Working with Mail

Once you have set up an account in the Mail app you can then start creating and managing your emails with it.

 On the main mail page, open an email and click on the **Reply**, **Reply all** or **Forward** buttons to respond

← Reply   ← Reply all   → Forward

 Open an email and click on the **Delete** button to remove it

🗑 Delete

Composing an email

To compose and send an email message:

 Click on this button to create a new message

+ New mail

 Click in the **To** field and enter an email address

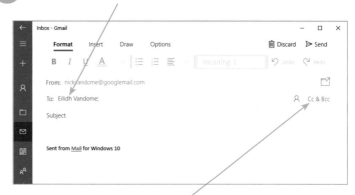

 Click on the **Cc & Bcc** link to access options for copying and blind copying

The email address can either be in the format of myname@email. com, or enter the name of one of your contacts from the People app (see pages 202-203), and the email address will be entered automatically

Don't forget

Contacts that are added automatically as email recipients are taken from the People app, providing there is an email address connected to their entry.

5 Enter a subject heading and body text to the email

Bcc:

Impressive cathedral

Thought you might like this!

6 Click on the **Insert** button on the top toolbar in the new email window and select one of the options, such as **Pictures**

| Format | **Insert** | Draw | Options |

📎 Files   ▦ Table   🖼 Pictures   🔗 Link   😊 Emoji

7 Click on a folder from which you want to attach the file, and click on the **Insert** button

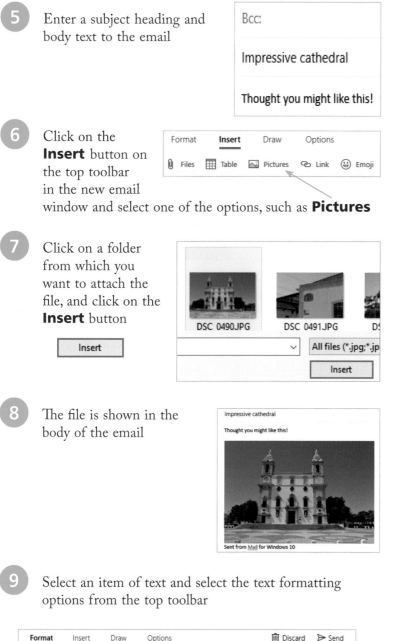

DSC 0490.JPG   DSC 0491.JPG   D!

Insert

All files (*.jpg;*.jp

Insert

When composing an email, or at any other time, press the Windows key (WinKey) and the period/ full stop key to access a panel for adding emojis (graphical symbols) to an item. This can also be used with other messaging apps. This is a new feature in the Windows 10 November 2019 Update.

8 The file is shown in the body of the email

Impressive cathedral

Thought you might like this!

Sent from Mail for Windows 10

9 Select an item of text and select the text formatting options from the top toolbar

| **Format** | Insert | Draw | Options | 🗑 Discard   ➤ Send

B *I* U ∨ ☰ ☰ ☰ ∨   Heading 1   ∨   ↺ Undo   ↻ Redo

10 Click on this button to send the email

➤ Send

Chatting with Skype

Skype is one of the premier services for free video and voice calls (to other Skype users) and instant messaging for text messages. It can now be incorporated into your Windows 10 experience and used to keep in touch with family, friends and work colleagues at home and around the world.

If the Skype button is not available on the Start menu, the app can be downloaded from the Microsoft Store.

Hot tip

If you are signed in to your PC with your Microsoft Account details then you should be able to use Skype without having to first sign in.

 Click on the **Skype** button on the Start menu

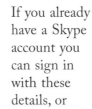 If you already have a Skype account you can sign in with these details, or

with your Microsoft Account details. Click on **Create a new account** to create a new Skype account

Once you have entered your Skype login details you can check your speakers, microphone and webcam for voice and video calls. Click on the **Sign In** button

Recent conversations are listed in the left-hand panel, or contacts can be selected to start a new conversation (see next page)

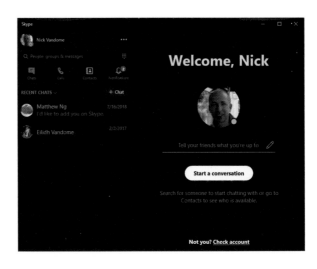

5 Click on this button to view your Skype contacts. Tap on one to start a voice or video call or text message

6 Click in the **People, groups & messages** Search box to look for other Skype contacts

7 Select a contact and click in this box to start a text conversation. Click on this button to **Send** the message

8 Select a contact and click on the phone button to make a voice call, or the video button to make a video call

Don't forget

When you create a text conversation with one of your contacts in Skype, it will continue down the page as you respond to each other.

Don't forget

When you add someone as a contact you have to send them a contact request, which they must accept to become one of your contacts.

Beware

Do not accept requests from people you don't know. If you receive one of these, click on **Decline** when they send you a request.

Finding People

An electronic address book is always a good feature to have on a computer, and with Windows 10 this function is provided by the People app. This not only allows you to add your own contacts manually; you can also link to any of your online accounts, such as Gmail or iCloud, and import the contacts that you have there. To do this:

If the People app is being used for the first time there will be a page with an option to add contacts from an existing account, such as Google or iCloud. If an account has already been added for the Mail app then this can be used, and there is also an Import contacts option for importing from another account.

1. Click on the **People** app on the Start menu

2. The current contacts are displayed. Double-click on a contact to view their details that have been entered

Hot tip

You can also select accounts to add to the People app from the Homepage when you first open it.

3. Click on a letter at the top of a section to access the alpha search list. Click on a letter to view contacts starting with the selected letter

Hot tip

To delete a contact, right-click on their name in the Contacts list and click on the **Delete** button to remove it.

4. Click on the **Settings** button to add new accounts from which you want to import contacts, such as a Gmail or an iCloud account (in the same way as setting up a new email account). Click on the **Add an account** button to add the required account. The contacts from the linked account are imported to the People app

Adding contacts manually

As well as importing contacts, it is also possible to enter them manually into the People app:

 Click on the **New contact** button on the top toolbar

Enter details for the new contact, including name, email address and phone number

Hot tip

Once a contact has been added, select it as in Step 2 on the previous page and click on this button to edit the contact's details.

🖉 Edit

Click on the Down arrow next to a field to access additional options for that item

Mobile phone ⌄

▢ Mobile

⌂ Home

🖼 Work

▤ Company

▦ Pager

Hot tip

When a contact has been selected, click on the pin icon on the top toolbar and select either **Pin to Taskbar** or **Pin to Start** to pin the contact here. More than three contacts can now be pinned in this way.

Click on the **Save** button at the bottom of the window to create the new contact

Using the Calendar

The Calendar app can be used to record important events and reminders. To view the calendar:

The Calendar interface has been updated in the Windows 10 November 2019 Update.

1 Click on the **Calendar** app on the Start menu

2 Click on the **Settings** button

3 The Settings include an option for selecting a background design for the calendar

Settings

Background

4 Click here to view the calendar in **Day**, **Week**, or **Month** mode

Accounts can be added to the Calendar app in the same way as for the Mail and People apps.

5 Click on these buttons to move between months (or swipe left or right on a touchpad)

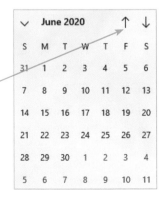

Adding events

Events can be added to the calendar and various settings can be applied to them, such as recurrence and reminders.

1 Click on a date to create a new event and click on the **New event** button

2 Enter an **Event name** and a **Location** at the top of the window

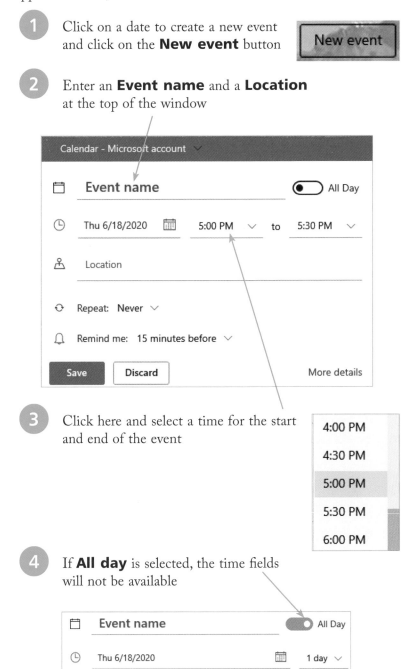

3 Click here and select a time for the start and end of the event

4:00 PM
4:30 PM
5:00 PM
5:30 PM
6:00 PM

4 If **All day** is selected, the time fields will not be available

Reminders can be set for calendar events, and these appear in the **Notification** area. Click on this box in Step 2 to set a time period for a reminder.

Events can also be added directly from the Taskbar. To do this, click on the current date and add the event details in the **Add an event or reminder** box. The date can be changed using the calendar that is above the **Today** box. This is a new feature in the Windows 10 November 2019 Update.

205

...cont'd

5 For a recurring event, click on the **Repeat** button at the top of the window

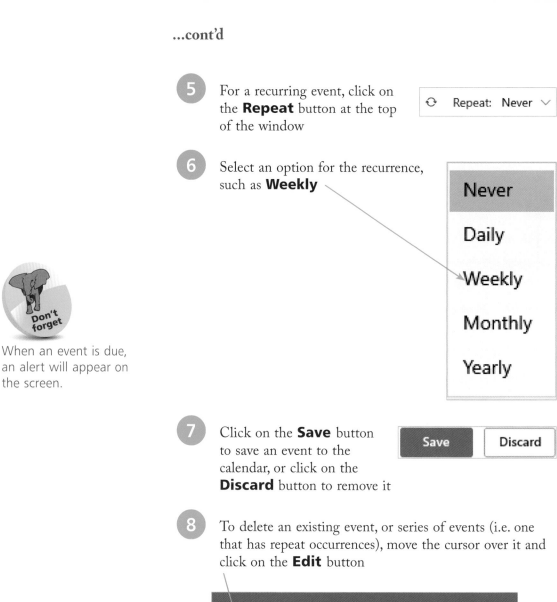

🔄 Repeat: Never ∨

6 Select an option for the recurrence, such as **Weekly**

Never

Daily

Weekly

Monthly

Yearly

When an event is due, an alert will appear on the screen.

7 Click on the **Save** button to save an event to the calendar, or click on the **Discard** button to remove it

Save   Discard

8 To delete an existing event, or series of events (i.e. one that has repeat occurrences), move the cursor over it and click on the **Edit** button

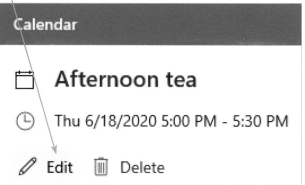

Calendar

🗓 **Afternoon tea**

🕐 Thu 6/18/2020 5:00 PM - 5:30 PM

✏ Edit   🗑 Delete

11 Networking and Sharing

Windows 10 has a built-in networking capability, for connecting to the internet and also sharing files between two (or more) computers.

208 Network Components

209 Connecting to a Network

210 Viewing Network Status

212 Nearby Sharing

214 Sharing Settings

215 View Network Components

216 Network Troubleshooting

The network adapter can be connected to the USB port, inserted in the PC card slot or installed inside your computer.

Ethernet adapters connect to a network hub, switch or wired router. Wireless adapters connect through a wireless router or a combination of router/switch.

You may already have some of these elements in operation, if you have an existing network running a previous version of Windows.

Network Components

There are numerous possibilities for setting up a home network. To start with, there are two major network technologies:

- **Wired** – e.g. Ethernet, using twisted pair cables to send data at rates of 10, 100 or 1000 Mbps (megabits per second).

- **Wireless** – using radio waves to send data at rates of 11 to 300 Mbps, or up to, in theory, 1 Gbps with the latest devices (although all of these are theoretical top speeds).

There is also a variety of hardware items required:

- **Network adapter** – appropriate to the network type, with one for each computer in the network.

- **Network controller** – one or more hub, switch or router, providing the actual connection to each network adapter.

There is also the internet connection (dial-up, DSL or cable), using:

- A modem connected to one of the computers.

- A modem connected to the network.

- Internet access incorporated into the router or switch.

Setting up the components

The steps you will need, and the most appropriate sequence to follow, will depend on the specific options on your system. However, the main steps will include:

- Install network adapters in the computers, where necessary (in most cases these will be preinstalled in the computer).

- Set up or verify the internet connection – this should be provided by your Internet Service Provider (ISP).

- Configure the wireless router or access point (this could involve installing software for the router, which may be provided on a CD or DVD. Some routers will be automatically recognized by Windows 10).

- Start up Windows on your PC.

Windows 10 is designed to automate as much of the network setup task as possible.

Connecting to a Network

You can connect your computers to form a network using Ethernet cables and adapters, or by setting up your wireless adapters and routers. When you start up each computer, Windows 10 will examine the current configuration and discover any new networks that have been established since the last start-up. You can check this, or connect manually to a network, from within the Wi-Fi settings from the Network & Internet section of Settings. To do this:

1 Access the **Settings** app and click on the **Network & Internet** button

Network & Internet
Wi-Fi, airplane mode, VPN

2 Drag the Wi-Fi button **On**. Under the **Wi-Fi** heading, click on one of the available networks

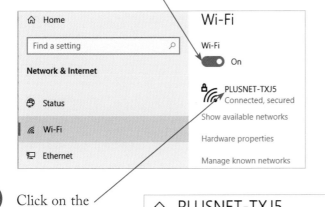

3 Click on the network and drag **On** the **Connect automatically when in range** button

⌂ PLUSNET-TXJ5

Connect automatically when in range

On

4 The selected network is shown as **Connected**. This is also shown in the Notification area, by right-clicking on the **Network** button and selecting **Open Network**

PLUSNET-TXJ5
Connected, secured

The most common type of network for connecting to is the internet.

If your network is unavailable for any reason, this will be noted in Step 2.

Viewing Network Status

Once you have connected to a network, and usually the internet too, you can view your current network status. To do this:

 Access the **Settings** app and select **Network & Internet**. Click on the **Status** button in the left-hand panel

 The currently connected network is shown under **Network status** (this will normally be your Wi-Fi connection to the internet)

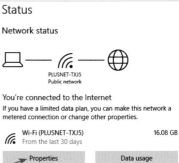

 Click on the **Properties** button to view the settings for the current network connection

4 The properties for the current network are displayed. Check **On** the **Private** option to make your PC discoverable to other devices on a trusted network; e.g. your home network

5 To reduce data usage, drag the **Set as metered connection** button from **Off** to **On**. This can be used if you have a limited data Wi-Fi service, and Windows will make system changes to reduce overall network traffic

6 On the main Status page, under **Advanced network settings**, click on **Change adapter options** for your network adapter

Advanced network settings

Change adapter options
View network adapters and change connection settings.

7 Details of the network connections are displayed

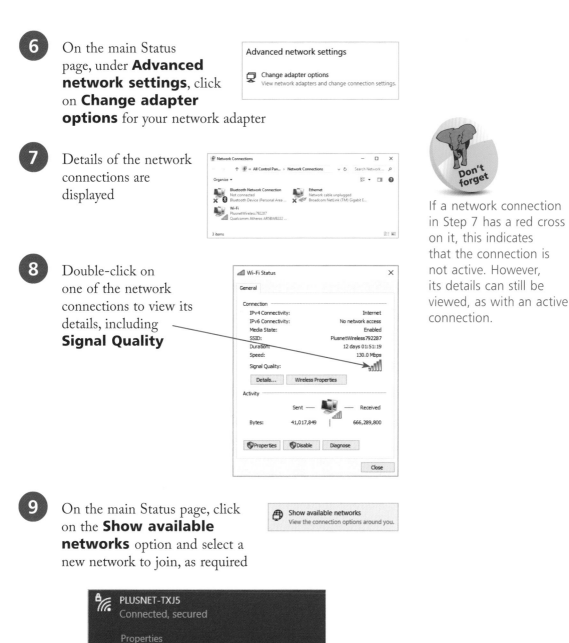

Don't forget

If a network connection in Step 7 has a red cross on it, this indicates that the connection is not active. However, its details can still be viewed, as with an active connection.

8 Double-click on one of the network connections to view its details, including **Signal Quality**

9 On the main Status page, click on the **Show available networks** option and select a new network to join, as required

Show available networks
View the connection options around you.

Nearby Sharing

The HomeGroup feature that was previously available with Windows 10 is no longer used in the November 2019 Update. Instead, Nearby sharing can be used to share files wirelessly, either using Bluetooth or Wi-Fi. As the name suggests, the computer with which you want to share files has to be relatively close to the one that is sharing the content. Also, the other device has to support Nearby sharing; i.e. be running a compatible version of Windows 10. To use Nearby sharing:

1 Access the Settings app and click on the **Shared experiences** button within the **System** section

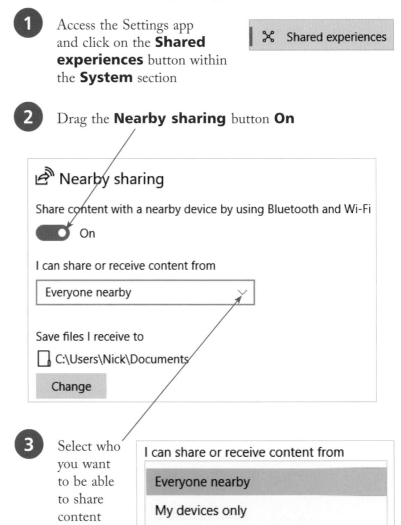

2 Drag the **Nearby sharing** button **On**

Don't forget

If your PC does not have Wi-Fi or Bluetooth capability, the Nearby sharing option will not be available.

3 Select who you want to be able to share content with your PC. It can be everyone, or only your own devices; i.e. ones on which you have signed in with your Microsoft Account details

4 Under the **Save files I receive to** heading, click on the **Change** button to select a new location

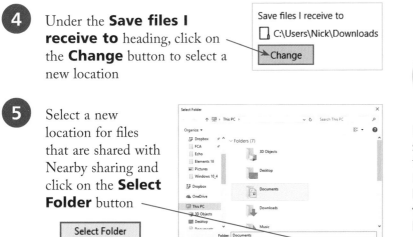

5 Select a new location for files that are shared with Nearby sharing and click on the **Select Folder** button

If a new folder has been selected for storing files downloaded using Nearby sharing, this will be listed under the **Save files I receive to** heading.

Sharing files

Once Nearby sharing has been set up it can be used to share files wirelessly with other compatible devices. To do this:

1 Access the Settings app and select **System > Notifications & actions > Add or remove quick actions** and drag the **Nearby sharing** button **On**

2 Open the Action Center and click on the **Nearby sharing** button so that it is blue

The **Share** option in Step 3 can also be used to share a selected item in a variety of other ways, including email and social media sites.

3 Open File Explorer and select a file. Click on the **Share** button in the **Share** section of the Scenic Ribbon

4 Click on the person's name with whom you want to share the file

Sharing Settings

Within the Network and Sharing Center there are also options for specifying how items are shared over the network. To select these:

1 Open **Settings > Network & Internet > Wi-Fi** and click on the **Change advanced sharing options** link, under the **Related settings** heading

Related settings

Change adapter options

Change advanced sharing options

2 Select sharing options for different networks, including Private, Guest or Public, and All networks. Options can be selected for turning on network discovery so that your computer can see other computers on the network, and for file and printer sharing

If you are sharing over a network you should be able to access the Public folder on another computer (providing that network discovery is turned On). If you are the administrator of the other computer you will also be able to access your own Home folder, although you will need to enter the required password for this.

Advanced sharing settings

↑ ⚙ « Network and Sharing Center › Advanced sharing settings   Search Control P...

Change sharing options for different network profiles

Windows creates a separate network profile for each network you use. You can choose specific options for each profile.

Private (current profile)

Network discovery

When network discovery is on, this computer can see other network computers and devices and is visible to other network computers.

◉ Turn on network discovery
☑ Turn on automatic setup of network connected devices.
○ Turn off network discovery

File and printer sharing

When file and printer sharing is on, files and printers that you have shared from this computer can be accessed by people on the network.

◉ Turn on file and printer sharing
○ Turn off file and printer sharing

Save changes   Cancel

3 Click on these arrows to expand the options for each network category

Change sharing options for different network profiles

Windows creates a separate network profile for each network you use. You can choose specific options for each profile.

Private (current profile)

Guest or Public

All Networks

Public folder sharing

When Public folder sharing is on, people on the network, including homegroup members, can access files in the Public folders.

○ Turn on sharing so anyone with network access can read and write files in the Public folders
◉ Turn off Public folder sharing (people logged on to this computer can still access these folders)

View Network Components

You can also view the components of the network in File Explorer. To do this:

1 Open File Explorer and click on the **Network** library

2 To view the shared items offered by a particular computer (for example, NICKLAPTOP), double-click on the associated icon

3 Double-click to view the contents of networked folders

Public files and folders, plus those belonging to the currently active user, are available to access. Items can be copied here for sharing purposes.

Don't forget

The Public folder on your own computer can be used to make items available to other users on the network.

Network Troubleshooting

 Open **Settings** >
Network & Internet
> **Status** and click on
the **Network troubleshooter** link

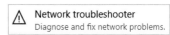

⚠ Network troubleshooter
Diagnose and fix network problems.

For more Windows 10
troubleshooting options,
see page 219.

216

 Click on the option that most closely matches your
network problem

← 🖳 Windows Network Diagnostics   ×

What type of networking problems are you having?

Windows tested your Internet connection and verified that you are able to access some
websites. Are you looking for help with a different issue?

→ I'm trying to reach a specific website or folder on a network

→ I'm having a different problem
   Show me other network troubleshooting options.

                                                                    Cancel

---

3 Most options have additional selections that can be made
to try to solve the problem. Click on these as required

← 🖳 Windows Network Diagnostics   ×

Choose the networking issue to troubleshoot

→ Allow other computers to connect to this computer

→ Connect to your workplace using DirectAccess

→ Use a specific network adapter (for example, Ethernet or wireless)

                                                                    Cancel

---

12 System and Security

Windows 10 includes tools
to help protect your online
privacy, troubleshoot
common problems, maintain
your hard drive, protect
against malicious software,
and back up your content.

218 Privacy

219 Troubleshooting

220 System Properties

222 Clean Up Your Disk

224 Windows Update

227 Backing Up

228 System Restore

230 Windows Security

Privacy

Online privacy is a major issue for all computer users, and Windows 10 has a number of options for viewing details about your personal online privacy.

 Open the **Settings** app and click on the **Privacy** button

<table>
<tr><td>🔒</td><td>Privacy
Location, camera, microphone</td></tr>
</table>

 Drag these buttons **On** or **Off** to allow advertising more specific to you, let websites provide local content based on the language being used by Windows, and let Windows track apps that are launched to make the search results more specific

General

Change privacy options

Let apps use advertising ID to make ads more interesting to you based on your app activity (Turning this off will reset your ID.)
○ Off

Let websites provide locally relevant content by accessing my language list
⬤ On

Let Windows track app launches to improve Start and search results
⬤ On

Show me suggested content in the Settings app
⬤ On

Know your privacy options

Learn how this setting impacts your privacy.
Learn more
Privacy dashboard
Privacy statement

Click on **Privacy statement** in Step 2 to view Microsoft's Privacy statement (this is an online statement and, by default, is displayed within the Edge browser).

3 Click on **Privacy dashboard** to view details on the Microsoft website about how ads are used online and in Windows 10 apps

4 Click on the **Sign In With Microsoft** button to manage your own personal privacy settings, including browsing data, search history and location data

Click on **Learn more** in Step 2 to view further details about general privacy settings and options within Windows 10.

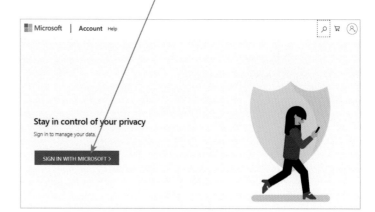

Microsoft | Account Help

Stay in control of your privacy
Sign in to manage your data.

SIGN IN WITH MICROSOFT >

Troubleshooting

On any computing system there are always things that go wrong or do not work properly. Windows 10 is no different, but there are comprehensive troubleshooting options for trying to address a range of problems. To use this:

1 Open the **Settings** app, select **Update & Security** and click on the **Troubleshoot** button

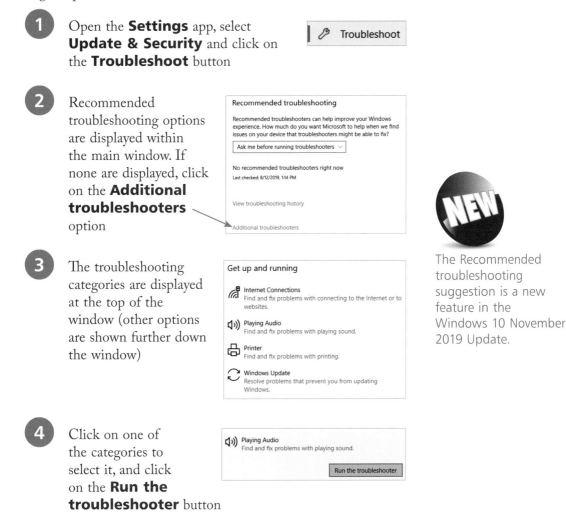

2 Recommended troubleshooting options are displayed within the main window. If none are displayed, click on the **Additional troubleshooters** option

3 The troubleshooting categories are displayed at the top of the window (other options are shown further down the window)

4 Click on one of the categories to select it, and click on the **Run the troubleshooter** button

5 Any issues for the selected item are displayed, along with options for trying to fix the issue

The Recommended troubleshooting suggestion is a new feature in the Windows 10 November 2019 Update.

System Properties

There are several ways to open the System Properties, and view information about your computer:

- Select **Settings** > **System** > **About**, or

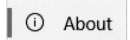

- Press the **WinKey** + the **Pause/Break** keys, or

- Right-click **This PC** in the File Explorer Navigation pane, then select **Properties** from the menu, or

- Right-click on the **Start** button, then select **System** from the Power User menu.

The main System panel (About) provides the Windows 10 edition, processor details, memory size and device name.

Device Manager

1 Select **Settings** > **System** > **About** and click on **System info** under **Related settings.** Then, click on **Device Manager** to list all of the hardware components that are installed on your computer

Related settings

BitLocker settings

System info

🛡 Device Manager

You may be prompted for an administrator password or asked for permission to continue, when you select some Device Manager entries.

2 Select the › symbol to expand that entry to show details

3 Double-click any device to open its properties

Intel(R) HD Graphics Properties

General Driver Details Events Resources

Intel(R) HD Graphics

Device type: Display adapters
Manufacturer: Intel Corporation
Location: PCI bus 0, device 2, function 0

Device status

This device is working properly.

OK   Cancel

Device Manager

File Action View Help

⌄ 🖥 Nicklaptop
 › 🔊 Audio inputs and outputs
 › 🔋 Batteries
 › 🟦 Bluetooth
 › 🖥 Computer
 › 💾 Disk drives
 › 🖥 Display adapters
 › 💿 DVD/CD-ROM drives
 › 🖱 Human Interface Devices
 › IDE ATA/ATAPI controllers
 › Imaging devices
 › ⌨ Keyboards
 › 🖱 Mice and other pointing devices
 › 🖥 Monitors
 › 🖧 Network adapters
 › Other devices
 › 🖨 Print queues
 › Processors
 › SD host adapters
 › Software devices
 › 🔊 Sound, video and game controllers
 › Storage controllers
 › System devices
 › Universal Serial Bus controllers

4 Select the ⌄ symbol to collapse the expanded entry

5 Select the Driver tab and select **Update Driver** to find and install new software

6 Select **Disable Device** to put the particular device offline. The button changes to **Enable Device**, to reverse the action

Intel(R) HD Graphics Properties

General Driver Details Events Resources

Intel(R) HD Graphics

Driver Provider: Intel Corporation
Driver Date: 12/21/2015
Driver Version: 10.18.10.4358
Digital Signer: Microsoft Windows Hardware Compatibility Publisher

Driver Details   View details about the installed driver files.
Update Driver   Update the driver for this device.
Roll Back Driver   If the device fails after updating the driver, roll back to the previously installed driver.
Disable Device   Disable the device.
Uninstall Device   Uninstall the device from the system (Advanced).

OK   Cancel

Enable Device

Click on the **Roll Back Driver** button (if available) to switch back to the previously installed driver for a device, if the new one for it fails.

Clean Up Your Disk

 In File Explorer, right-click the **C:** drive and click on the **Properties** option

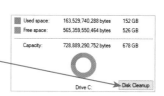

2 Click on the **Disk Cleanup** button

3 Disk Cleanup scans the drive to identify files that can be safely removed

You can have more than one hard disk on your computer.

4 All of the possible files are listed by category, and the sets of files recommended to be deleted are marked with a tick symbol

 Make changes to the selections, clicking **View Files** if necessary to help you choose

6 Select the **Clean up system files** button, to also include these, then select **OK**

7 Deleted files will not be transferred to the Recycle Bin, so confirm that you do want to permanently delete all of these files. The files will be removed and the disk space will become available

...cont'd

When a file is written to the hard disk, it may be stored in several pieces in different places. This fragmentation of disk space can slow down your computer. Disk Defragmenter rearranges the data so the disk will work more efficiently.

1 In the File Explorer, right-click on the **C:** drive and click on the **Properties** option

> > 🎞 Videos
> > 💻 Acer (C:)

Properties

Don't forget

Spellings are localized.

2 Select the **Tools** tab and click on the **Optimize** button

> 💿 Acer (C:) Properties ✕
>
> | Security | | Previous Versions | | Quota |
> | General | Tools | | Hardware | Sharing |
>
> Error checking
> This option will check the drive for file system errors.
> 🛡Check
>
> Optimize and defragment drive
> Optimizing your computer's drives can help it run more efficiently.
> Optimize

3 The process runs as a scheduled task, but you can select a drive and select **Analyze** to check out a new drive

> 🎛 Optimize Drives — ☐ ✕
>
> You can optimize your drives to help your computer run more efficiently, or analyze them to find out if they need to be optimized. Only drives on or connected to your computer are shown.
>
> Status
>
> | Drive | Media type | Last run | Current status |
> |---|---|---|---|
> | 🖴 Acer (C:) | Hard disk drive | 7/22/2019 2:00 PM | OK (0% fragmented) |
>
> 🛡Analyze 🛡Optimize
>
> Scheduled optimization
>
> **On**
> Drives are being optimized automatically.
> Frequency: Weekly
>
> 🛡Change settings
>
> Close

Hot tip

Only disks that can be fragmented are shown. These can include USB drives that you add to your system.

4 Click the **Optimize** button to process the selected disk drive. This may take between several minutes to several hours to complete, depending on the size and state of the disk, but you can still use your computer while the task is running

223

Windows Update

Updates to Windows 10 and other Microsoft products are supplied regularly to help prevent or fix problems, improve the security or enhance performance. The way in which they are downloaded and installed can be specified from the Settings app:

 Access the **Settings** app and click on the **Update & Security** button

> ↻ **Update & Security**
> Windows Update, recovery, backup

 Click on **Windows Update**

> **Update & Security**
>
> ↻ Windows Update

An icon for alerting you to available updates can be placed on the Taskbar, rather than having to check within the Settings app each time. To set this up, access **Settings** > **Update & Security** > **Windows Update** > **Advanced options** and check **On** the **Show a notification when your PC requires a restart to finish updating** option. When an update is available, the icon on the Taskbar will display an orange dot. This is a new feature in the Windows 10 November 2019 Update.

③ Click on the **Check for updates** button to see details of any updates that are waiting to be installed

> **Windows Update**
>
> ↻✓ You're up to date
> Last checked: Yesterday, 1:51 PM
>
> Check for updates

 There are a range of options available on the main Windows Update page, for managing the way that updates are performed on your PC or laptop (see pages 225-226)

> **Windows Update**
>
> ↻ Updates available
> Last checked: 8/18/2019, 4:15 PM
>
> ⏸ Pause updates for 7 days
> Visit Advanced options to change the pause period
>
> 🕐 Change active hours
> Currently 8:00 AM to 5:00 PM
>
> 🕐 View update history
> See updates installed on your device
>
> ↻⚙ Advanced options
> Additional update controls and settings

5 Click on the **Pause updates for 7 days** option to stop updates being installed for seven days

 Pause updates for 7 days
Visit Advanced options to change the pause period

6 A yellow icon appears on the Windows Update page, indicating that updates have been paused. Click on the **Resume updates** button to resume them again

Windows Update

Updates paused
Your device won't be up to date while updates are paused.
Updates will resume on 8/28/2019

Resume updates

Updates can be paused for up to 35 days, in seven-day periods; i.e. the seven-day pause can be activated five times until the update has to be installed. This is a new feature in the Windows 10 November 2019 Update.

7 Click on the **Change active hours** button to specify a time period for when updates cannot be performed; e.g. the normal hours of use for your computer. Click on the **Change** button to edit the times

Change active hours
Currently 8:00 AM to 5:00 PM

⌂ Change active hours

Set active hours to let us know when you typically use this device. We won't automatically restart your device during this time.

Automatically adjust active hours for this device based on activity
 Off

Current active hours: 8:00 AM to 5:00 PM   Change

Based on your daily activity, we recommend using the following active hours:
From 8:00 AM to 5:00 PM

Drag the **Automatically adjust active hours for this device based on activity** button **On** in Step 7 to enable Windows 10 to select active hours based on your usage. This is a new feature in the Windows 10 November 2019 Update.

8 Enter the new times for the active hours and click on the **Save** button

Active hours

Set active hours to let us know when you typically use this device. We won't automatically restart it during active hours, and we won't restart without checking if you're using it.

Start time

| 7 | 00 | AM |

End time (max 18 hours)

| 6 | 00 | PM |

| Save | Cancel |

225

...cont'd

 Click on the **View update history** button to view details of updates that have been installed

 View update history
See updates installed on your device

⌂   View update history

Uninstall updates

Recovery options

Update history
∨ Feature Updates (1)
  Windows 10 Insider Preview 19008.1 (vb_release)
  Successfully installed on 10/25/2019
  See what's new in this update

∨ Quality Updates (1)
  Cumulative Update for Windows 10 Version Next
  Successfully installed on 10/27/2019

 Click on the **Advanced options** button and drag the buttons **On** or **Off** for the relevant options, including receiving details of other Microsoft products when Windows is updated, how restarts are handled after an update and showing the Windows Update notification icon on the Taskbar

Advanced options
Additional update controls and settings

⌂   Advanced options

Update options

Receive updates for other Microsoft products when you update Windows
🔘 On

Download updates over metered connections (extra charges may apply)
🔘 Off

Restart this device as soon as possible when a restart is required to install an update. Windows will display a notice before the restart, and the device must be on and plugged in.
🔘 Off

Update notifications

Show a notification when your PC requires a restart to finish updating
🔘 Off

Pause updates

Temporarily pause updates from being installed on this device for up to 7 days. When you reach the pause limit, your device will need to get new updates before you can pause again.

Pause until
Select date ∨

Hot tip

Click in the **Pause updates** box to select a specific date for pausing updates being installed, rather than the seven days in the pause option on page 225.

Backing Up

Backing up your data is an important task in any computer environment, and in Windows 10 this can be done from within the Settings app. To do this:

1 Access the **Settings** app and click on the **Update & Security** button

Update & Security
Windows Update, recovery, backup

2 Click on the **Backup** button

↑ Backup

3 Drag the **Automatically back up my files** button **On** to back up your files whenever the external drive is

Backup

Back up using File History
Back up your files to another drive and restore them if the originals are lost, damaged, or deleted.

Automatically back up my files
⬤ On

More options

connected. After the initial backup, each further one will be incremental; i.e. only new files that have been added or changed will be backed up, not the whole system

4 Click on the required external drive

Select a drive

Seagate Slim Drive (E:)
63.6 GB free of 465 GB

5 Click on the **More options** button in Step 2 to view backup options. Click on the **Back up now** button to perform a manual backup

⌂ Backup options

Overview
Size of backup: 0 bytes
Total space on Seagate Slim Drive (E:) (E:): 465 GB
Backing up your data...
Back up now

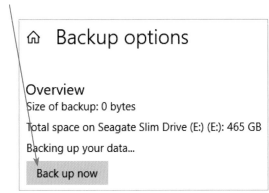

Don't forget

If a backup is being set up for the first time, there will be an option to **Add a drive** after the Backup option in Step 2 has been accessed.

Don't forget

The **Recovery** option in **Update & Security** has a **Reset this PC** option that can be used to reinstall Windows and select which files you want to keep.

System Restore

Windows 10 takes snapshots of the system files before any software updates are applied, or in any event once every seven days. You can also create a snapshot manually. The snapshots are known as Restore Points and are managed by System Restore.

1 From the Control Panel, open **System** under **System and Security** and select **System protection**

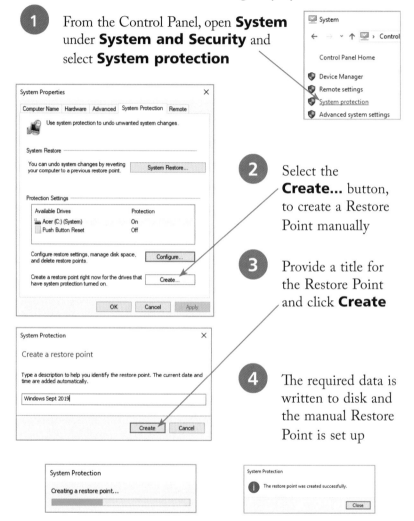

Hot tip

System Restore returns system files to an earlier point in time, allowing you to undo system changes without affecting your documents, email, and other data files.

2 Select the **Create...** button, to create a Restore Point manually

3 Provide a title for the Restore Point and click **Create**

4 The required data is written to disk and the manual Restore Point is set up

Beware

System Restore is not intended for protecting personal data files. For these you should use Windows Backup (see page 227).

Using Restore Points

The installation of a new app or driver software may make Windows 10 behave unpredictably or have other unexpected results. Usually, uninstalling the app or rolling back the driver (see page 221) will correct the situation. If this does not fix the problem, use an automatic or manual Restore Point to reset your system to an earlier date when everything worked correctly.

1 Select **System protection** and
click the **System Restore...** button

| System Restore... |

2 By default, this will offer to undo the most recent change.
This may fix the problem

System Restore

Restore system files and settings

System Restore can help fix problems that might be making your
computer run slowly or stop responding.

System Restore does not affect any of your documents, pictures, or
other personal data. Recently installed programs and drivers might be
uninstalled.

< Back   Next >   Cancel

You can also run
**System Restore
from Safe Mode**, the
troubleshooting option.
Start up the computer
and press **F8** repeatedly
as your computer
reboots, to display the
boot menu, then select
Safe Mode.

3 Otherwise, click a suitable item to use as the Restore Point

System Restore

Restore your computer to the state it was in before the selected event

Current time zone: GMT Daylight Time

Date and Time	Description	Type
8/19/2019 12:19:24 PM	Windows Sept 2019	Manual
8/15/2019 1:26:35 PM	Automatic Restore Point	System

Scan for affected programs

< Back   Next >   Cancel

If the selected Restore
Point does not resolve
the problem, you can try
again, selecting another
Restore Point.

4 Follow the prompts to restart the system using system
files from the selected date and time

Windows Security

The Windows Security app, which is preinstalled with Windows 10, can be used to give a certain amount of protection against viruses and malicious software. To use it:

 Select **Settings** > **Update & Security** > **Windows Security**

 The Windows Security options are listed in the window, under the **Protection areas** heading

Windows Security

Windows Security is your home to view and manage the security and health of your device.

Open Windows Security

Protection areas

Virus & threat protection
Actions recommended.

Account protection
Actions recommended.

Firewall & network protection
No actions needed.

App & browser control
No actions needed.

Device security
No actions needed.

Device performance & health
Reports on the health of your device.

Family options
Manage how your family uses their devices.

 Click on one of the Protection areas categories to view its options

← ≡

⌂ ♡ ⊗ (ᵗᵖ) ▭ ⊟ ♡ ⅋

🖥 Device security

Security that comes built into your device.

▦ Core isolation

Virtualization-based security protects the core parts of your device.

Core isolation details

🔆 Secure boot

Secure boot is on, preventing malicious software from loading when your device starts up.

Learn more

Standard hardware security not supported.

Learn more

4 Click on the **Open Windows Security** button on the main security page to open the Windows Security app

Windows Security

Windows Security is your home to view and manage the security and health of your device.

Open Windows Security

5 Click each item to view its options and use the left-hand toolbar to move between the sections. Click on the **Home** button to return to this page

Using a firewall

A firewall can be used to help protect your network from viruses and malicious software. To do this:

1 Click on the **Firewall & network protection** option on the Windows Security Homepage

2 Click one of the network names

3 Drag the **Microsoft Defender Firewall** button **On** to activate the firewall for the selected network

🖩 Domain network

Networks at a workplace that are joined to a domain.

Active domain networks

Not connected

Microsoft Defender Firewall

Helps protect your device while on a domain network.

⬤━ On

Hot tip

The Microsoft Defender Firewall can be used to provide a level of protection against malicious software and viruses.

231

Don't forget

Firewall is on by default in Windows 10, but you can turn it off if you have another firewall installed and active.

...cont'd

Protecting against viruses

The Windows Security center can be used to give a certain amount of protection against viruses and malicious software. To do this:

 On the Windows Security Homepage and click on the **Virus & threat protection** option

Virus & threat protection
Tamper protection is off. Your device may be vulnerable.

 Click on the **Quick scan** button to scan your system for viruses

🛡 Virus & threat protection

Protection for your device against threats.

🕑 **Current threats**

No current threats.
Last scan: 8/14/2019 1:22 PM (quick scan)
0 threats found.
Scan lasted 1 hours 18 minutes
14976 files scanned.

Quick scan

Scan options

Allowed threats

Protection history

3 As the scan progresses, any threat will be noted and options for dealing with them listed; e.g. remove or quarantine the item(s)

🛡 Virus & threat protection

Protection for your device against threats.

🕑 **Current threats**

Quick scan running...
Estimated time remaining: 00:00:14
5219 files scanned

Cancel

Don't forget

Malware (malicious software) is designed to deliberately harm your computer. To protect your system, you need up-to-date antivirus and anti-spyware software. Windows Defender can provide this, and you can also install a separate antivirus app.

Index

A

Access Action Center
   With swipe gesture   16
Access administration tools
   With keyboard shortcut   15
Access an app's toolbar
   With swipe gesture   16
Access Cortana
   With keyboard shortcut   15
   With touchpad   16
Access File Explorer
   With keyboard shortcut   15
Access Quick access
   With keyboard shortcut   15
Access the Desktop
   With keyboard shortcut   15
Access the Ease of Access options
   With keyboard shortcut   15
Access the Settings app
   With keyboard shortcut   15
Access the Start menu
   With keyboard shortcut   15
Access the Task Manager
   With keyboard shortcut   15
Access the Task View
   With swipe gesture   16
Action Center   44.   *See also* Notifications
Active hours   225
Adding a phone   41
Adding notes to web pages   189
Adding users.   *See* Users: Adding
Address bar   96, 136-137
Address book.   *See* People app
Add to compressed folder   163
Adjacent block selection   146
All apps
   Grid   80
   Viewing   80
All files and folders   147
Alternative programs   153
App list
   Minimizing   80
Apps.   *See also* Windows 10 apps
   About   72-73
   Alphabetic list   80
   Buying   87
   Classic   78
   Closing   77, 79
   Installing   90
   Maximizing   77
   Menus   77
   Microsoft Store   84-88
   Microsoft Store apps   72
   Minimizing   77
   Moving   76
   Pin to Start menu   82
   Pin to Taskbar   83
   Reinstalling   88
   Restrictions   69
   Searching for   81
   Switching
      Accessing with touch   16
   Uninstalling   91
   Using   76-77
   Windows 10 apps   72
   Windows classic apps   72
Apps view.   *See* All apps
Arrange icons   107
Arrange windows   100
Associated programs   153

B

Back button   96
Background
   Setting   110
Backing up   227
Backtrack file operations   160
Bing   75
Bookmarking web pages   188
Braille   122
Browser.   *See* Microsoft Edge browser
Burn to disc   151
Buying apps   87
Bypass the Recycle Bin   157

C

Calendar   204-206
   Adding events   205-206
Cascade windows   100
Changing views in File Explorer   140
Checkbox   95
Clean up your disk   222-223
Close an app
   With keyboard shortcut   15

Close window	98, 108
Collapse	135
Color themes	
Changing	114-115
Command button	95
Compare windows	103
Compressed folders	163
Compressed item properties	164
Conflicts with files and folders	152
Connect new devices	
With keyboard shortcut	15
Contacts.	See People app
Continuum	16
Control icon	96-97
Control menu	97, 108
Control Panel	17
Pinning	17
Copy files and folders	148
Cortana	64-67
Searching with	65-66
Setting up	64
Using	65-67
Create compressed folder	163
Create folders	158
Cut, Copy, Paste files and folders	150

D

Date and time functions	124
Deactivate Recycle Bin	157
Delete files and folders	154
Desktop	36, 137
Accessing	25
Accessing with shortcuts	36
From the keyboard	15
Desktop icons	107, 119
Desktops	
Adding	39
Deleting	39
Details view in File Explorer	141
Device Manager	221
Dialog box	95
Dimmed option	94
Disk Defragmenter	223
Display Menu bar	94
Display the Lock screen	
With keyboard shortcut	15
Display the thumbnails on the Taskbar	
With keyboard shortcut	15
Documents	136, 162
Drag files and folders	149

E

Ease of Access	122-123
From login screen	20
From the keyboard	15
High contrast	123
Magnifier	123
Narrator	122
Edge browser.	See Microsoft Edge browser
Emojis	199
Ethernet	208
Explorer.	See File Explorer
Exploring drives	134
Extract files and folders	164

F

Family Safety	69
File Explorer	126-144
Close	142
From the keyboard	15
Libraries	128
Open	126
Quick access	132-133
Scenic Ribbon	129
View	138
File properties	161
Files and folders	
Burn to disc	151
Conflicts	152
Copy	148
Create	158
Cut, Copy, Paste	150
Delete	154
Drag	149
Move	148
Rename	159
Search	162
Select	146-147
File type	158
Filtering in File Explorer	142
Firewall	231
Focus assist	44-45
Folder options	95, 144
Folders on the Start menu	35
Forward	96
Frequently used apps	
On the Start menu	26
Full screen mode	30

G

Game Bar	55
Gaming	179-180
Achievements	179
Activity alert	180
Activity feed	179
Clubs	180
Friends list	180
Game Bar	180
Messages	180
My games	179
Parties	180
Trending	180
Gestures	16
GMail	196
Graphical User Interface (GUI)	8
Grayed option	94
Groove Music app	174
Group by	107
Group by in File Explorer	143
Groups	
On the Start menu	32
Editing names	33
Naming	33

H

Hard disk drive	131
Hide menu bar	94
Hotmail renamed	196

I

Install app	90
Internet Explorer	182

K

Keyboard	
Delete key	154
Keyboard shortcuts	15

L

Language	
Display	64
Speech	64
Libraries	128-130, 135, 141
Properties	161
Library	
File menu	129
Home menu	129
Manage menu	130
Menu options	130
Share menu	130
View menu	130
Library location	128
Library tools	129
Light Theme	114
Live Preview	106
Live Tile functionality	89
Calendar	89
Groove Music	89
Mail	89
Money	89
News	89
People	89
Photos	89
Sport	89
Local account	
Signing in with	21
Location	131
Locking the screen from the keyboard	15
Locking your computer	20
Lock screen	20
Settings	116-117
Logging in	20-21
Login settings	21

M

Mail	196-199
Accounts	196
Formatting	199
POP3 account	196
Sending	198-199
Setting up	196-197
Malware	232
Maximize	96-97
Menu bar	94

Microsoft Account   18
    Creating   18-19
    Email address   68
    Prompted to create   18
    Services   18
Microsoft Defender Firewall   231
Microsoft Edge browser
    About   182
    Accessing Favorites   191
    Adding notes   189-190
    Bookmarking pages   188
    Browsing history   191
    Clear history   191
    Clutter-free printing   193
    Customized themes   185
    Downloads   191
    Find on page   194
    Homepage button   184
    Hub   191
    Importing Favorites   184
    InPrivate browsing   194
    Menu options   194
    Print   194
    Reading list   191-192
    Reading view   193
    Set aside tabs   187
    Setting a Homepage   184
    Settings   194
    Smart address bar   183
    Tab previews   186
    Tabs   185
    Zoom   194
Microsoft Store
    About   84-86
    Buying apps   87
    Downloaded apps   88
    Home   86
    Ratings and reviews   85
    Reinstalling apps   88
    Viewing your apps   88
Microsoft Store apps   73
Microsoft website for Windows 10   14
Microsoft Windows.   See Windows
Minimize   96
Mixed Reality Portal   74
Mouse pointer   96
Move files and folders   148
Move window   97
Movies and TV
    Viewing   176
MS-DOS   8
Multimonitor support   97
Multiple windows   104-105
Music
    Playing   175

Navigation panes   131, 138-139
    Details pane   139
    Preview pane   139
Nearby sharing   48, 212-213
Network   135
    Components   208
    Troubleshooting   216
    View components   215
Night light   47
Non-adjacent files selection   147
Notepad   94
Notifications   42-43
    Settings   43

OneDrive
    Adding items to File Explorer   167
    Adding items to OneDrive online   168
    Adding items to the OneDrive app   168
    Online   166
    Overview   166
    Personal Vault   166
    Settings   169
Open files   153
Open window   100, 108
Optimizing folders   130
Outlook   196

Paint 3D   178
Partial sequence selection   147
Pausing updates   225-226
Peek   101
Peek at desktop   101
People app   202-203
    Adding contacts manually   203
    Finding   202-203
    Pinning contacts   203
Permanently erase files   156
Personalization   110-111
Personalize Windows   119
    Desktop icons   119

Photos
    App   170-173
    Draw button   172
    Editing   172-173
    Importing   170
    Viewing   170-171
Picture password   22
PIN   22
Pin to Start menu   82
Pin to Taskbar   83
Power off button   20
Power options   24
Precision touchpads   16
Preinstalled Windows   14
Preserve file types   159
Printers
    Adding   49

Q

Quick access folder
    In File Explorer   132-133
    Pinning items   133

R

Radio button   95
Recycle Bin   155, 222
    Bypass   157
    Deactivate   157
    Empty   156
    Permanently erase files   156
    Resize   157
    Restoring files   155
Redo   160
Removing users.   See Users: Removing
Rename files and folders   159
Resize window   99
Restart   37
    For updates   37
Restore Point   228
Restore window   96, 98, 103
Reveal file extensions   158
Ribbon.   See Scenic Ribbon
Ruler   96
Run function   90

S

Safe Mode   229
Save your work   108
Scenic Ribbon   94, 96, 129-130
Screen brightness   42
Screen resolution   120
Search
    Files and folders   162
Search box   96, 131
Searching   62-63
    Asking a question   63
    Over your computer   63
    Text search   62
Select files and folders   146
Sequential files selection   146
Settings   46-61
    Accessing   46
    Accounts   53
        Access work or school   53
        Email & accounts   53
        Family & other users   53
        Sign-in options   53
        Sync your settings   53
        Your info   53
    Adding to the Taskbar   46
    Apps   52
        Apps & features   52
        Apps for websites   52
        Default apps   52
        Offline maps   52
        Startup   52
        Video playback   52
    Cortana   58
    Devices   49
        AutoPlay   49
        Bluetooth & other devices   49
        Mouse   49
        Pen & Windows Ink   49
        Printers & scanners   49
        Touchpad   49
        Typing   49
        USB   49
    Ease of Access   56
        Audio   56
        Closed captions   56
        Color filters   56
        Display   56
        Eye control   56
        High contrast   56
        Keyboard   56
        Magnifier   56

Mouse	56
Mouse pointer	56
Narrator	56
Speech	56
Text cursor	56
Gaming	55
Captures	55
Game Mode	55
Xbox Game Bar	55
Xbox Networking	55
Network & Internet	50
Airplane mode	50
Dial-up	50
Ethernet	50
Mobile hotspot	50
Proxy	50
Status	50
VPN	50
Wi-Fi	50
Personalization	51
Background	51
Colors	51
Fonts	51
Lock screen	51
Start	51
Taskbar	51
Themes	51
Phone	49
Privacy	58
Account info	59
Activity history	59
Automatic file downloads	59
Background apps	59
Calendar	59
Call history	59
Camera	59
Contacts	59
Diagnostics & feedback	58
Documents	59
Email	59
File system	59
General	58
Inking & typing personalization	58
Location	59
Messaging	59
Microphone	59
Notifications	59
Other devices	59
Pictures	59
Radios	59
Speech	58
Tasks	59
Videos	59

Search	57
Permissions & History	57
Searching Windows	57
System	47-48
About	48
Battery	48
Clipboard	48
Display	47
Focus assist	47
Multi-tasking	48
Notifications & actions	47
Power & sleep	47
Projecting to this PC	48
Remote Desktop	48
Shared experiences	48
Sound	47
Storage	48
Tablet mode	48
Time & Language	54
Date & time	54
Language	54
Region	54
Speech	54
Update & Security	60
Activation	61
Back up	61
Delivery Optimization	60
Find my device	61
For developers	61
Recovery	61
Troubleshoot	61
Windows Insider Program	61
Windows Update	60
Sharing files	213
Shortcut keys	15, 94, 102, 108, 150
Shortcuts for keyboard	15
Show desktop	101
Show desktop icons	119
Shutting down	37
Affecting other users	70
From the Start button	37
Side-by-side windows	104-105
Sign-in options	20-21
Single file or folder selection	146
Skype	200-201
Contacts	201
Downloading	200
Making calls	201
Sleep	37
Snap Assist	102-103
Snapshots with System Restore	228
Sort by option in File Explorer	143
Sorting files in File Explorer	141
Sound	118

Specifications
    For running Windows 10   12
Spotify   175
Stack windows   100
Start button   24-25
    Functionality   24-25
    In previous versions   73
    Shutting down from   37
    Using   24
Start menu   13, 26-31
    Creating folders   35
    Customizing   30-31
    Frequently used apps   26
    Full screen mode   30
    Power button   26
    Removing items   31
    Resizing tiles   34
    Shutting down from   37
    Transparency   51
    Versions   28
    Working with groups   32-33
Storage   121
Structure of the Desktop   36
Structure of window   96
Surface Pro tablet   13
Swiping gestures
    For touch devices   16
Switch users   70
Switch windows   106
System Properties   220
    Device Manager   221
System Restore   228-229
    For creating Restore Points   228

T

Tablets   13, 30
Tabs   95
    Using in Microsoft Edge   185
Taskbar   36, 127
    From the keyboard   15
    Notification area   36
    Pinning items   83
    Transparency   51
    Viewing open windows   36
Taskbar buttons   98
Task Manager
    From the keyboard   15
    Performance   92
    Processes   92
Task View   38-39
    For viewing open apps   38

Task View button
    Showing or hiding   38
Text Document file   158
Text size   56
Themes   112-113
This PC
    Folders   135
    For accessing Properties   220
This PC folder   131
Tile windows   100
Time and date functions   124
Time controls   69
Timeline   40
Title bar   96
Touch for Windows 10   16
Touchscreen devices   13, 16
Transparency   51, 97
Troubleshooting
    Network   216
    Windows   219
Turning off   37

U

Undo   100, 160
Uninstalling apps   91
Unpinning apps   82-83
Update Assistant
    For obtaining Windows 10   14
Updates
    Restarting   37
USB device   134
Users
    Adding   68-69
    Removing   69
Using Restore Points   228

V

Viewing open apps   38-39
View network components   215
Viruses
    Protecting against   232
Voice calls
    With Skype   200-201
Voice search
    With Cortana   65-66

W

Web browser.	*See* Microsoft Edge browser
Web filtering	69
Web searches	63
Windows	8
History	8
Previous versions	8-9
Windows 8	9
Windows 10	
About	9
For touch	16
Installing	14
Obtaining	14
Windows 10 apps	72, 74-75
3D Viewer	74
Alarms & Clock	74
Calculator	74
Calendar	74
Camera	74
Closing from the keyboard	15
Groove Music	74
Mail	74
Maps	74
Messaging	74
Microsoft Edge	74
Microsoft News	74
Microsoft Store	74-75
Mixed Reality Portal	74
Money	74
Movies & TV	75
OneDrive	75
OneNote	75
Paint 3D	75
People	75
Photos	75
Reader	75
Settings	75
Snip & Sketch	75
Sports	75
Stickies	75
Toolbars	
Accessing with touch	16
Voice Recorder	75
Weather	75
Xbox Console	75
Windows 10 interface	12-13
Windows 10 November 2019 Update	9
About	10-11
Windows 10 Update Assistant	9, 14
Windows apps	73
Windows Hello Face	21
Windows Hello Fingerprint	21

Windows Live Search.	*See* Bing
Windows logo key	15
Windows security	230-232
Windows structure	96
Windows Update	60, 224-226
Active hours	225
For obtaining Windows Update	14
Pausing updates	225
Windows updates	
Restarting	37
Windows XP	8
WinKey shortcuts	15
WinZip	163
Wireless network	208
WordPad	94, 96
Wrong password	
When signing in	20

X

Xbox Console Companion app	179-180

Z

Zipping folders	163
Zoom	
With Microsoft Edge	194